FIRST LADIES

OF THE

POSTER

FIRST LADIES
OF THE
POSTER

The Gold Collection

Laura Gold

With an Introduction by Jack Rennert

POSTERS PLEASE, INC.
NEW YORK

Photo credit for "Déjeuner sur l'herbe" by Edouard Manet
and "Birth of Venus" by Sandro Botticelli: Erich Lessing/Art Resource, N.Y.

Published and distributed by
THE POSTER ART LIBRARY
a division of
POSTERS PLEASE, INC.
601 West 26th Street
New York, New York 10001

ISBN 0-9664202-0-9

Designed by Michael Mendelsohn
Typesetting and electronic paging by Harry Chester Inc.
Printed and bound in Japan by Dai Nippon Printing Co.

Contents

Women: Symbols and Subjects in   vi
Turn-of-the-Century Posters by Jack Rennert

Preface by Laura Gold   xi

PRODUCTS & SERVICES   1

WINES & LIQUORS   29

FOOD & BEVERAGES   37

BICYCLES & CARS   47

PUBLICATIONS   57

APPAREL   79

SPORTS & RECREATION   85

TRAVEL   93

ENTERTAINMENT   99

PERFORMING ARTS   105

EVENTS   123

DECORATIVE ART   135

Artists' Biographies   142

Index   147

Women

Symbols and Subjects
in Turn-of-the-Century Posters

I t would be utter folly to assert that the use of the female form as a motivating force in art sprang to life in the poster milieu of late 19th-century France. The image of Woman, both as subject and symbol, has been both an obsession and inspiration to artists and collectors alike ever since the world began trading in the commerce of beauty. Whether one looks to the allegorical symbolism of Botticelli's *Birth of Venus* or to Manet's nude as part of the pastoral landscape in *Déjeuner Sur l'Herbe,* it is abundantly clear that the female form is one that attracts and holds the eye of the viewer. Plainly stated, sex sells. So what else is new?

The use of women as symbols and subjects in posters, therefore, was simply a natural progression, a continuation of an established practice. This is amply displayed in the magnificent works of Alphonse Mucha (the ethereal stoicism of *F. Champenois Imprimerie-Editeur* and the languid beauty of *Salon des Cent/XXme Exposition,* nos. 36 and 192), Privat Livemont (*Cacao Van Houten,* no. 54, reveling in austere splendor) or Georges de Feure (the unapproachable elegance of *Paris-Almanach,* no. 79). The exceptional charm, grace, and elegance of these idealized women are beyond question. But they remain *objets d'art,* unattainable allegories without much, if any, connection to the world about them.

This is not meant as a criticism. Not in the least. These masterpieces shine as examples of the exceptional mastery these artists commanded. The *fin de siècle* poster, however, is most notable for bringing that artistry to street level and, in the process, becoming a mirror of the society which bustled about them. "Whereas the Impressionists had wanted to catch the moment on the wing, advertising artists had to capture attention at a glance. . . . Whenever possible, the product advertised was combined with the erotic appeal of a feminine image" (*France, Fin de Siècle* by Eugen Weber, p. 155).

But the image of femininity itself was in a profound state of flux. The end of the 19th century "was a turning point in the long history of women, as if the traditional deck had been reshuffled. The old tensions were still present — between work (at home or in the shop) and family, between the domestic ideal and social utility, between the world of appearances, dress and pleasure and the world of subsistence, apprenticeship, and the practice of a profession . . . But the cards were dealt out differently, and new stakes had been added to the game. If women's life were transformed, how can we find out what they thought about the transformation?" (*A History of Women in The West: IV. Emerging Feminism from Revolution to World War,* edited by Geneviève Fraisse and Michelle Perrot, p. 3).

One answer lies in the fact that posters furnished us with a reflection of these times. They are images of empowerment, providing us with the transformation from the classical images of beauty that we have seen up to this point. Women are no longer merely objects on display, but are instead shown beginning to take charge

Sandro Botticelli. *The Birth of Venus.* 1484.

(Uffizi Gallery, Florence)

Edouard Manet. *Déjeuner sur l'herbe.* 1863.

(Musée d'Orsay, Paris)

of their situations and liberating themselves. What initially seem to be bright, light-hearted designs actually offer a penetrating glimpse into the daily life of the Victorian woman and her gradual emancipation from the stifling constraints placed upon her. We now see the goddess stepping down off her pedestal and becoming an active participant in her own life.

As opposed to an ideal figure, cast up purely for viewing pleasure, images display women going about their day-to-day business. Certainly it may appear to our theoretically sophisticated eye that the images are somewhat pedestrian, but they represent the first time where products directly appealed to the consumer-fueled tastes of the emerging middle-class woman. Posters, the most democratic art, showed her goods, services, and a whole lifestyle that was not just a daydream, but a goal which just might be attainable.

We see images of daily turn-of-the-century life, be it purchasing a corset (Alfred Choubrac's *Corsets Baleinine,* no. 120, which refreshingly shows styles suited to *every* woman), grocery shopping (the charming *Pêcheurs Réunis* from Adrien Barrère, no. 65), choosing cookware (Francisco Tamagno's *Aluminite,* no. 11) or picking out the best possible lamp oil (the fresh-faced, jubilant envoys of accessible femininity executed by Jules Chéret for *Saxoléine,* nos. 26 and 28).

Jules Chéret. *Saxoléine.* 1890.

(The Gold Collection)

We are presented with women stepping out of the confining traditional roles in which they were cast and exercising their new-found liberation. We see them taking to the roads on bicycles (the most widespread graphic icon of female liberation, shown, for example, in H. Gray's *Cycles Buffalo,* engaged in nothing less than a pedal-powered bison hunt, no. 73) and getting behind the wheels of automobiles (not one, but two female motorists are featured in *Benzo Moteur* by Chéret, no. 22, and a woman brazenly thumbs her nose at the trailing pack of male drivers in Marcellin Auzolle's delightful *Auto Barré,* no. 76).

Posters show women expanding their horizons even farther from their standard posts, taking the helm of a boat (Adolfo Hohenstein's *Monaco,* no. 135) or extending their freedom to the skies (an anonymous work for *Le Petit Parisien,* no. 111). We are

provided with glimpses into women's burgeoning, nascent sexual freedom. No longer the radiant, vaunted untouchables of Mucha nor the giddy party girls so wonderfully produced by Chéret, they are instead rendered with an honest sensuality that is at once attainable and evocative (see the unapologetic pulchritude of H. Gray's *Cycles Sirius,* no. 69, or the sensuous self-indulgence of *Fleurs de Mousse* by Leopold Metlicovitz, no. 7).

Of all the poster artists who created these magnificent images of the emerging modern woman, one in particular stands head and shoulders above the rest: Jules Chéret. One can never overstate the important role which he played in the advancement of poster design, as well as his place in bringing women to the forefront of these images. As an innovative printer, as well as a designer, he established the methods which allowed color lithography to be effectively and economically viable for such a mundane and widespread distribution medium as the poster. To truly appreciate the revolutionary changes in the cityscape wrought by Chéret's innovations, one needs to look at Paris B.C. (Before Chéret). The following few examples will quickly illustrate the point:

Whether selling a house, announcing the opening of a play, or presenting Baba, the 11-foot-high elephant, posters before Chéret were basically black-and-white woodblock engravings with some stock ornamentation. The poster for the Bonne Bière de Mars, dating around 1810, is a hand-colored woodcut engraving — this was as good as color posters got before Chéret's lithographic innovations.

Additionally, if a single poster artist can be credited for utilizing spectacular women as a marketing device, that artist is once again Chéret. All the posters prior to his color extravaganzas, including his own earlier works, deposit the women as essential members of a family setting, or if she were to appear alone, it would be for women's wear, modestly clad from head to toe. To be sure, subsequent artists such as Pal, Grün, H. Gray, Tamagno and others, who specialized in bringing their works to life with buxom and vivacious women, were a reflection of the less stringent attitudes of their times. But a good deal of credit must be given to Chéret, the master whose practices propped open the door through which they entered, providing them with inspiration and freedom to explore the possibilities of their medium. Without Chéret's wistful groundwork, their designs would have appeared scandalous and an affront to politesse instead of a natural, accepted progression.

All of these wonderful works clearly demonstrate the reflective nature behind their production. The intriguing speculation that these posters create, however, comes from what is not so immediately evident:

To what degree did they plant the seeds of female emancipation? At the *fin de siècle,* the effect of the poster was pervasive and profound, much as television is today. The poster during this period was responsible for informing the emerging middle-class woman of the possibilities available to her. Granted, these images showed a world that was seriously attainable to only a small percentage of that population. But when a shop girl or a working-class wife saw the image of a woman hoisting an aperitif bottle (as in Leonetto Cappiello's rosily intoxicating *Nuyens's Menthe,* no. 45) or attending a gala ripe with possibilities (lusciously realized by Pal in *Théâtre de l'Opéra,* no. 191), their minds certainly must have begun to mull over the possibility of testing the waters of freedom. Since these posters exposed the message of liberation to a wider range of the female population, one has to wonder to what extent these images were a motivating force behind the drive for material possession and, ultimately, liberation.

It is interesting to note the differences between the French representations of women in posters at the turn of the century and their counterparts in the United States. Briefly stated, the French were miles ahead of the Americans, displaying their women as a liberated, societally active force (clearly mounted in Mucha's *Job,* no. 2 and Chéret's *Vin Mariani,* no. 42), whereas their American sisters, although featured in the images, remained demure, decorous, "in their place," if you will. (See Louis J. Rhead's *Sunday Press,* no. 94 or Will H. Bradley's *Bradley/His Book/June,* no. 106). In France, the women are shown integrating themselves into the bustling world about them. The American poster women on the other hand, while used as potent selling devices, are socially correct and ornamental when they appear. Though it is tempting to draw any number of conclusions from this difference, the most accurate assumption one can make is that the French images went further towards instilling a greater yearning for this advertised freedom. No doubt, the puritanical influence of the American ideal also played a part here at home.

Of course, when gazing at these works, it is wonderfully simple to romanticize, to glance at a poster for the Folies-Bergère and be swept away with visions of elegance, music and romantic, flirtatious encounters. It's tempting to create an ideal by emphasizing the positive as we peer back through the mists of time. However, the truth of the matter is that ". . . it is good to remember how different it was. The past is another country. . . [filled with] the servant problem and the labor problem and the problem of foreign labor; the threat . . . of tourists defiling remote beauty spots . . . ; the cumbersome confinement of women's skirts; ringing coins to see if they sound true; dueling; the problem posed by walking amid cobble-stone, horse-droppings, mud, or dust; the ubiquity of horses and the noise they made; bad smells; the danger from food adulterated by private enterprise or else by swift natural decay before the age of refrigeration; the paucity of clean linen; the rankness and violence of political invective and much of private life" (Weber, *op. cit.,* p. 6). Then, as now, it was probably a welcome relief to be able to escape into a brightly-colored alternate world created by brilliant designers.

This book brings us some of the finest works from that time when posters were all the rage. It is awash with splendid images and vibrant colors, a window into a bygone era where a world of possibilities was just beginning to reveal itself to the women who craved an expanded role and broader boundaries than what their society was willing to offer. And though that world was far from perfect, it is a pleasure to be able to indulge in the visions of the artists who took it upon themselves to create one that was.

The Gold Collection is the culmination of more than three decades of Laura Gold's poster dealership at the Park South Gallery at Carnegie Hall. What is not as immediately obvious is the fact that Laura has chosen to retain these particular images in order to compile a singular, highly personal collection. She is, after all, a dealer. And an art dealer does not covet; an art dealer sells! It is therefore all the more remarkable that these treasures of the Golden Age of Posters were not only preserved, but cherished by her. For her abundant love of these images, for her boundless enthusiasm in sharing them with others and creating a legion of new poster enthusiasts–this book is evidence and extension of that–all of us in this field owe her a debt of gratitude. She is the consummate friend of the poster–and I'm honored to have been counted as a friend of Laura's for all these years.

* * *

I want to acknowledge the many individuals on our staff who have been most helpful in the realization of this volume, and I want to especially thank the editor, Judith A. Goldstein, our researcher, Tim Gadzinski, our photographer, Gunther Knopf, and our designer, Michael Mendelsohn. The care and professionalism of the Dai Nippon printing firm was crucial, and we appreciate especially the personal attention given every aspect of the production process by Mr. Tsuyoshi Maganuma of DNP America, Inc.

Finally, it is crucial at this point to acknowledge the lasting indebtedness which is owed to the poster collectors of the 1890s, who chose not to accumulate the fine art which had been created 100 years before, but instead to harvest the immediate art of the street which surrounded them on a daily basis. Sadly enough, all indications point to the fact that this type of *affichomanie* will never recur. Even with the current resurgence of poster collecting, the most sought-after pieces are the ones which were created in the past instead of the contemporary art created for today's consumers. Granted, the graphic art which dominates the world of poster advertising in this day and age is more often than not less than collectible. It is something of a shame, however, that all works are seemingly lumped together in a disposable heap. It's hard to imagine today's collectors sneaking about with razors, clandestinely liberating fresh images from the subway stops and papered walls throughout the city or, as at the turn of the century, bribing billposters not to paste them. Let us hope that, if nothing else, this book will provoke the creation of a discerning palate, effecting an awareness of the possibilities of the medium and instilling a desire to preserve today's posters alongside these established masterpieces.

— Jack Rennert
President, Posters Please, Inc.

Preface

T his is a personal collection.

The first question asked when I am interviewed is how I got started in this business. My background was in advertising and printing. I was a printing buyer for various magazines and Madison Avenue advertising agencies. In that capacity I gained knowledge of plate making, paper, inks, and lithography. I also acquired an appreciation of the techniques used in the development of commercial printing in the 1890s, which led to the evolution of the advertising poster.

In 1963 I took over the Park South Gallery at Carnegie Hall. It was not long before I found myself being pulled away from the paintings and watercolors and toward what I knew best: advertising and printing. Together they make a poster, and old posters seemed to call out to me. I marveled at the drawing of each plate, all done by hand, and was awestruck by the skill it took to print one color at a time, all to give the scenes and figures dimension, depth, and life. To me, the printing of some of these poster seemed to lift off the paper and soar! Old posters became a passion. I found my calling. I was a round peg in a round hole.

Along the way, the focus of my private collection became the story of women at the turn of the 20th century. Women emerging into the full force of life at the time. We see the female being used for commercial exploitation and, at the same time, coming out of the home and into the swirl of the Industrial Revolution, entering the social fabric of "La Belle Epoque".

This selection of images may not be as comprehensive as a historian or curator would prefer. For instance, I have two posters of the singer Eugenie Buffet (the original "little sparrow") but none for the singer Yvette Guilbert. I prefer the Metivet posters of Eugenie. By the same token, I have four posters for the dancer Loie Fuller (my favorite is by Georges de Feure) and none of Jane Avril. I've thought about this and realized it is a result of my attending a symposium in 1979 at the Virginia Museum in Richmond, Virginia titled "Loie Fuller: Magician of Light." She had an interesting life — starting out in a bar in Illinois and ending up as the toast of Paris. The life of Jane Avril just wasn't all that interesting to me.

I also have favorite artists: Steinlen and Pal. Steinlen for his humanity and hold on reality, Pal for the quality of his drawings on stones. These guys were simply the best. Along with Chéret they are well represented in this collection.

For me as a dealer, a source of great joy has been the privilege of building poster collections for others. Individuals who placed faith in me to find the very best images, in the best possible condition, acquired affordably. A collection of tennis posters for a midwestern tennis center; newspaper posters for the printing plant of a southern newspaper; fish posters for a New York fish distributor; posters only by certain artists, posters of a certain entertainer. And a host of individual pursuits such as jewelry, photography, dentistry, and lithographic presses. For all these, I have done my best.

A special remembrance goes to the late Mr. Kimio Doi of the Doi Camera Company in Japan. After interviewing dealers around the world for two years, he finally came to me and said "build my collection." Today his legacy is the finest collection of Mucha posters (in addition to his advanced acquisitions of jewelry

and paintings by the artist) in the world. His full collection will be housed in the Mucha Museum, under the stewardship of Kyoichi Taguchi, to open at the beginning of the 21st century in Sakai City, Japan. Mr. Doi was also responsible for my first visit to Japan in 1984 for the "Timeless Images" exhibition at the Isetan Museum of Art, Shinjuku, Tokyo, which contained the loan of many of my posters, several of which you'll find in this book.

It has been most gratifying to see my posters displayed on loan to other museums, including the Centre Pompidou in Paris, France; Metropolitan Museum of Art, New York City; San Diego Museum of Art, California; Nassau County Museum of Art, New York; Jane Voorhees Zimmerli Art Museum, New Jersey; Museum of Fine Art, Montreal, Canada; and the Suntory Museum, Osaka, Japan.

I have always considered myself to be an equal opportunity buyer. To this end, I have found myself sitting in plush auction rooms from New York and London to Geneva and Monte Carlo, in the organized mayhem of auction houses all over France, in private homes and chateaux right out of "the rich and famous," and in unheated shacks, garages, and barns. From fancy print galleries to funky flea markets in the countryside, I have seen posters right out of a vault (not having seen the light of day for a hundred years) and rolled-up old paper half-eaten by bugs with rat turd in the folds. From open-toed satin sandals to rubber boots in the mud, it has all been part of a wonderful experience.

I wish to thank D. J. Dougherty, my associate, for his unending understanding, patience, and commitment to me and to the gallery. And his wife, Karla, for her input and patience with both of us. And my children, Jack and Ruth, who as youngsters were allowed to practice ice-skating on the living room rug, but not allowed to bump into the rolled posters under the piano, and heeded the admonition. From the age of seven they knew the difference between a Mucha and a Chéret; no wonder they grew up with a tolerance for their mother's quirky quest and passion.

Because my collection is mostly French, my travels to that country as well as other European cities over the years have been many. I stopped counting when they exceeded 150. Along the way I have come to respect and appreciate the relationships that have developed with many dealers and auction houses. Among them, my compatriots, the "lady dealers who lunch" in Paris: Mireille Romand, Anne Martiniere, and Isabel Maurel. Also in France, the experts: Alain Weill, Florence Camard, Francoise LePeuve, Christophe Zagrodski. Commissaire-Priseur Maitre Louis Savot and his associate Michel Guedron, Orleans. Richard Barclay in London; Jean-Louis Lamot in Brussels; and the late Jiri Mucha in Prague. In the United States: Terry Shargel, Posters Please; Louis Bixenman, Poster America, both of New York City. Sarah Stocking Fine Vintage Posters, San Francisco; Elena Millie, Library of Congress, Washington, D.C. For assistance with this book, Chester Collins and Judy Goldstein.

Lucy Broido of Bryn Mawr, Pennsylvania, author of the *catalogue raisonné* of Jules Cheret, suggested 25 years ago that we have a goal of being together on the porch of some old age home, playing with posters, still feeling like young girls playing with paper dolls. It still sounds like a good idea.

Over the years, many clients have become friends and colleagues have become like family. They are too numerous to mention. Carnegie Hall has been a wonderful landlord from the beginning.

And last but not least, my mentor, Jack Rennert. This man, who is the most knowledgeable in the field of posters in all the world, has pulled me and pushed me; taken me with him, translated, and negotiated on my behalf, and encouraged me with the words "go for it — you can do it." His generosity, humor, and dedication are constant. For the past ten years he has encouraged me to do a book. When he finally said, "do it, and I will publish it" — well, here it is. I am everlastingly grateful that he has been my best friend.

Even though I am now a private dealer, the gallery remains a continuing source of great delight and interest. As never-before-seen images continually come to light, the joy of discovery is non-ending. The passion goes on.

Laura Gold.

Products & Services

The growth of the consumer-oriented economy stemming from the Industrial Revolution was in full swing during the Belle Epoque. As more jobs provided more spendable income, the demand for goods motivated private enterprise to satisfy the consumer's every need. Once basic needs were covered, marketers found it profitable to create new needs, ones consumers never knew they had. Posters were an ideal way to educate consumers about what they should want: fashionable clothes to wear, time and effort-saving products for the kitchen, laundry, and office—all pleasant but hardly necessary.

To convince consumers that fashion, status, and convenience were as valid reasons to buy as necessity, marketing experts soon discovered the persuasive technique of showing products being enjoyed by beautiful people in beautiful settings. Pretty women soon smiled out of billboards selling everything imaginable.

Paradoxically, this exploitative use of feminine appeal in the service of commerce led to women's greatest period of emancipation. While the average woman could hardly imagine herself a Venus de Milo, idealized and glamorized figures on posters were believable role models—ordinary women who attained a better lifestyle by using this laundry detergent or that lamp, this throat pastille or that new corset.

Women, in short, were becoming educated consumers, gaining confidence to make their own buying decisions. Posters, being a potent visual medium, played a crucial role in the process.

JULES-ALEXANDRE GRÜN
Hérold & Cie

1908; Herold & Cie.; Paris;
15½ x 23½ in / 39.4 x 59.6 cm

To advertise a printer, Grün assembles a collection of his own best-known posters printed by the firm and adds an unusual touch: The enthusiastic billposter is a young woman— as charming in her workaday way as the artist's usual nighttime revelers.

❶

▶

ALPHONSE MUCHA
Job

1898; F. Champenois, Paris;
40 x 59 in / 101 x 149.2 cm

In both of Mucha's posters for Job cigarette papers—this is the second; the first was done in 1896—he gives us women sensuously absorbed in the act of smoking. Here, the figure is full-length, her abandoned hair a dark echo of the pale fabric volumes of her gown. As she watches the lazy waft of smoke, even her toes curl deliciously in pleasure. The artist's meticulous craftsmanship can be seen in such details as the gown's clasp (of Mucha's own design), and in the way he worked the product name into the background pattern.

❷

IMP. F. CHAMPENOIS, 66, Boul⁴ S⁴ Michel, PARIS

◄

EUGENE GRASSET
Encre L. Marquet

1892; G. de Malherbe, Paris;
32 x 45 in / 80.7 x 114.4 cm

Quill pen in hand, the pensive young woman is looking for inspiration to write something lyrical in this fine, evocative design for a writing ink. Grasset adheres to the classic mode of portraying women as serenely composed and dignified. Only the fluttering hair and scurrying night clouds suggest any wild untamed thoughts.

❸

LUCIEN LEFEVRE
Laveine/Enlève Encre

1893; Chaix, Paris;
34½ x 43 in in / 87.6 x 122 cm

The writer has wisely donned special gloves to protect her hands from the mess of the quill and inkwell, but her dress has not escaped. Fortunately, the product quickly removes inkspots and other spills, as the maid demonstrates.

❹

ANONYMOUS
Fleur du Bouquet de Noce

Ca. 1900; Strobridge Litho, London;
33 x 45 in / 74 x 114.5 cm

In encouraging women to take better care of themselves and their appearances, poster advertising widened the female sphere beyond the strictly domestic to a world that was looking at—and interested in—them. Here, an English model, drawn in black crayon from a photograph, offers eye-contact endorsement of "Bridal Bouquet Bloom," a face and body lotion. This version of the poster is in French.

❺

ANONYMOUS
Formodol

Ca. 1901; printer not shown;
31½ x 47¼ in / 80 x 120 cm

A winning smile is a prerequisite for selling toothpaste, and this woman is flashing hers. The unknown artist has cleverly made the name of the product into a hat by adding a pair of fluffy ostrich plumes.

❻

JULES CHERET
L'Eau des Sirènes

1888; Chaix, Paris;
47½ x 68 in / 120.7 x 172.7 cm

In the 1880s poster art was just emerging from the drabness of letterpress announcements showing little but black type. Chéret's airy images were so startlingly bright and fresh on the walls of Paris that they attracted many admirers and earned his spritely women the appellation "Chérettes." It is not too far-fetched to say that they were instrumental in ushering in the golden age of posters; at the very least they were highly influential in making posters a major medium of commercial communication. In this rare uncensored version of this poster, Chéret's barebreasted sirens sing the praises of a haircoloring product named in their honor. Apparently, the mermaid quartet was too alluring for the Paris censors who were just beginning their efforts at this time. They refused to accept the poster until Chéret lengthened the hair to partly cover the offending flesh. All known copies of this poster are unsigned.

❽

◀
LEOPOLD METLICOVITZ
Fleurs de Mousse

1899; Moullot Fils, Marseilles;
30½ x 46½ in / 77.5 x 118 cm

One of the most natural products for a woman to be associated with is perfume. In this particularly inspired design by the indefatigable Italian posterist Metlicovitz the woman is enraptured by the fragrance, which is so potent that the artist imagines it attracts even butterflies. How could a woman resist such an appealing message?

❼

H. GRAY (HENRI BOULANGER)
L'Ovale

Ca. 1898; Courmont Freres, Paris;
38 x 51½ in / 95.9 x 130.8 cm

Even a lowly hairpin gains stature when sold by an elegant woman in sumptuous surroundings, and Gray provides a textbook example of how it's done. L'Ovale hairpins come in two versions—straight and slant-sided—but the product's superiority lies in its trademarked design: gently rounded heads and ends that are more comfortable to wear.

⑨

R. GAUTIER
La Plaque Electra

Ca. 1920; Via-Decor, Paris;
45 x 61 in / 114.4 x 154.2 cm

For "yesterday's" housewife polishing silver was a hellishly laborious task; "today" a dip in Electra solution will bring up the shine and sparkle without any rubbing. Labor-saving products like this were among the most welcome effects of the industrial epoch; individual inventors and large industrial combines alike put their effort into products that would lessen the drudgery of running a household.

❶⓿

►

FRANCISCO TAMAGNO
Aluminite

1903; B. Sirven, Toulouse;
38 x 52 in / 96.5 x 132.1 cm

This early 20th-century Paris cook couldn't be more pleased. Not only does her kitchen boast a gas range (most homes would run on wood- or coal-burning stoves for several more decades), but she's also been provided with a complete set of Aluminite flame-resistant cookware. It's not clear whether these splendid utensils are solid aluminum or some sort of aluminized porcelain, but they've garnered reassuring prizes at numerous World's Fairs.

❶❶

ANONYMOUS
Le Repassage Au Gaz

Ca. 1894; Camis, Paris;
31 x 47 in / 78.5 x 119.5 cm

This poster recommends to the efficient
housewife a way of keeping things humming
while ironing: Instead of having to wait for a
cooled-off iron to reheat on the stove, she can
now use a little gas-fired stand whose direct
flame will do the job in seconds. The unknown
designer gives it the standard before-and-after
treatment, but the dividing line is handled very
tastefully and blended with the ornate frame.
A commendable promotion by the gas
company.

ANONYMOUS
La New Home

Ca. 1894; G. Masure, Bruxelles;
24 x 32.5 in / 63 x 80 cm

A humorous approach to selling a sewing
machine, worthy of a Norman Rockwell, by an
unknown Belgian artist. The machine, with its
international gold medals and Yankee name
suggesting new world-modernity, is so easy to
use that Granny can mend the mischief-
maker's pants right on him.

❶❸

▶

LEONETTO CAPPIELLO
Pianos Ortiz & Cusso

1903; Vercasson, Paris;
14.5 x 21 in / 36.9 x 53.4 cm

Here's a Spanish piano maker ordering a
Cappiello poster from Paris, although there
were competent posterists right in Barcelona.
Why? Because Cappiello would give his figures
so much elan and exuberance that piano
playing appears as pure joy.

❶❹

HENRI THIRIET
Machines à Coudre Peugeot

Ca. 1890; G. De Malherbe, Paris;
16 x 27¼ in / 40.6 x 69.2 cm

Before plunging into the exciting new automobile
manufacturing field in 1899, Peugeot was involved in
designing and building sewing machines for the domestic
trade; the company even won a prize at the 1889 Paris
World Fair, as the poster proclaims while showing us a
glimpse of the factory. This fine composition anticipates
Art Nouveau in its ornamental framing and delicate pastel
tones. More importantly, the image of a woman bent in the
eyestraining tedium of needle and thimble has been
replaced by a light, airy scene in which she sews with
comfort and ease.

❶❺

ANONYMOUS
Compagnie Singer Nähmaschinen

Ca. 1902; Société d'Affiches et de Réclames Artistiques, Genève;
31¼ x 47¼ in / 87 x 120 cm

One of the most durable trademarks associated with the
emancipation of women from tedious hand labor is the
Singer sewing machine, instantly recognizable in every
civilized country on the globe. The basic design of the
machine shown in this poster remained virtually unchanged
for at least half a century. Knowing that the product won
the Grand Prize at the 1900 Paris World's Fair adds to the
sewer's satisfaction and confidence. This is a German-
language version of the poster printed in Switzerland.

❶❻

▶

PAL (JEAN DE PALEOLOGUE)
Eyquem

Ca. 1898; Gaby & Chardin, Paris;
39½ x 55 in / 100.3 x 139.7 cm

Secretarial work was one of the first non-menial
employment opportunities for women in the labor market
created by the Industrial Revolution, and countless
thousands of girls began to acquire office skills as a normal
part of their education. This poster is for an early copying
machine, showing that the clerk can handle it with ease
while keeping her white cuffs spotless. Pal gave her a
winning smile and restrained allure.

❶❼

EUGENE VAVASSEUR
Hammond

1904; Arts Industriels, Paris;
15¼ x 32 in / 38.7 x 81.3 cm

In the 1880s the notion of a working woman immediately brought to mind a seamstress. By the first half of the 1900s, however, that image was supplanted by the secretary-typist—not simply a job but a profession and definitely a notch up on the social scale. Here, the typist is the center of world attention, represented by a range of exotically attired viewers. They are marveling at her Hammond typewriter whose ability to type any language and alphabet—even complex Chinese, Japanese, Arabic and Russian characters—has apparently won it a gold medal at the 1904 World's Fair in St. Louis.

❶❽

EMILE BERCHMANS
La Lampe Belge

Ca. 1896; A. Bernard, Liege;
38¼ x 26½ in / 97.2 x 67.3 cm

For the L&B Company, a Belgian manufacturer of kerosene lamps and heaters, Berchmans creates a domestic scene of considerable charm. The baby may safely play with the lamp because it's "inexplosible," leaving the mother free to read while her young daughter experiments at the stove in the background.

❶❾

►
AUGUSTE ROUBILLE
Spratt's Patent Ltd.

Ca. 1909; Lemercier, Paris;
45 x 61 in / 114.3 x 154.9 cm

Roubille uses a restrained yet warm style to show a happy mistress dispensing Spratt's treats to her clamoring canines. You can see the caricaturistic bent which showed up in the cartoons the artist contributed to humor magazines and in posters for Paris cabarets and revues. Spratt's was a major producer of food for pets and farm animals, based in England but with branches in several countries. Here, it advertises dog food for its French customers.

❷⓿

JULES CHERET
Benzo-Moteur

1900; Chaix, Paris;
34½ x 49 in / 87.6 x 124.5 cm

In 1900 cars were still pretty much a hobby for the venturesome. That meant mostly men, but Chéret shows one daring young woman at the wheel in the foreground and another in the smaller background image. The poster is for one of the first European brands of gasoline, sold at the time in canisters at general and hardware stores.

❷❷

PAL (JEAN DE PALEOLOGUE)
A La Place Clichy/Exposition de Blanc

1899; Caby & Chardin, Paris;
39¼ x 55¾ in / 99.7 x 139 cm

Pal's portrayals of women were always flattering, nearly worshipful: perfect bodies, perfect faces, classic beauty. But where artists such as Mucha or Privat Livemont idealized women, Pal, with his realistic attention to detail, gave them a decidedly solid, earthly quality: These are women of flesh and blood. It's not clear whether Pal's design shows two salesgirls at the Place Clichy White Sale packing up merchandise or a satisfied customer showing off her purchase at home, but in either case the women and the ruffled bed linens are equally appealing.

❷❸

◄

PAL (JEAN DE PALEOLOGUE)
Rayon D'Or

1895; Paul Dupont, Paris;
31¼ x 47¼ in / 79.3 x 119.6 cm

Rarely has a product so humdrum as a kerosene lamp been promoted with such uninhibited zest—but then Pal, given free rein to his imagination, could be relied on to come up with something featuring one of his incomparably alluring nymphs every time. The secret of his success is the fact that even though he makes it clear in some way—such as the gossamer wings here—that these are purely imaginary spirits, the loving care with which he draws every curve and flesh tone gives them a sensuality much too solid for make-believe. Puritans who might otherwise object to ordinary nudity were usually willing to make an exception for fairies, angels and the like, and Pal took better advantage of this double standard than anyone.

❷❶

HENRI THIRIET
Exposition de Blanc/à la Place Clichy

1898; De Vaugirard, G. De Malherbe, Paris;
52 x 36¼ in / 132.1 x 92.1 cm

A saleswoman at the Place Clichy White Sale shows a discerning customer some fine
bed linens. Thiriet makes the women's appearances and attitudes so charming and
gives the sheets themselves such sumptuous volumes that purchasing what is
essentially a household requirement seems as delightful as choosing a new dress.

❷❹

ANONYMOUS
Motricine

Ca. 1901; Courmont Freres, Paris;
39 x 55¹/₂ in / 99 x 141 cm

Careening recklessly down the road at speeds surely in excess of 15mph, the early motoring couple gives nary a thought to mechanical trouble because they have trusty Motricine in the gas tank. At this time cars were still considered a hobby for eccentrics: You had to enjoy barreling down dusty country lanes where cows and geese were often the only other traffic, endure the weather in open autos, and in the absence of service stations, occasionally locate a blacksmith shop that might sell you a can of gasoline if you needed it. Brava to the plucky passenger here!

❷❺

JULES CHERET
Saxoléine

1896; Chaix, Paris;
15 x 22¹/₂ in / 38.1 x 56.8 cm

Chéret's decade-long campaign for Saxoléine lamp oil is something of an advertising milestone. Each of the ten successive annual images contains a woman and a lamp; the only thing that changes is their mutual position. Sometimes the lamp is on the right, sometimes on the left; sometimes it is on a tall stand, other times on a small table; and of course, the color of the dresses and lamp shades also vary. Still, it takes a talent to be able to make the ten images look distinct from each other and make them interesting enough so that some people actually looked forward to see what next year's Saxoléine poster would look like.

❷❻

C. MORIGET
Appareils & Accessoires Pour La Photographie

Ca. 1897; P. Moreau, Nantes;
38 x 49¹/₂ in / 96.5 x 125.7 cm

A winsome picture-taker—perhaps even a professional photographer—advertises a camera store in Nantes. Appropriately, her face is a photographic likeness. What elevates this design beyond the commonplace is the skilled handling of the typography which serves as the framework of the composition.

2 7

JULES CHERET
Saxoléine

1900; Chaix, Paris;
33¹/₄ x 48¹/₂ in / 84.5 x 123.2 cm

Long before advertising science began to talk of product recognition, Chéret was creating it with his Saxoléine posters. He started out by creating a homey atmosphere with warm, friendly colors around the lamp; he then placed an attractive homemaker in close relation to the lamp and let her show pleasure at having such a bright light to illuminate the room. The product itself—a bottle of kerosene—is not shown. But Chéret knew that women would aspire to the beauty and high spirits of his model.

2 8

R. HEM
Aux Fabriques de Genève/ E. Billard

Ca. 1899; Kossuth, Paris;
47¼ x 63 in / 120 x 160 cm

Within the device of a gold ring set with diamonds, a jeweler's wares are displayed for the pleasure of a slender young beauty whose finely portrayed face may be the brightest gem here. An admirable design by a regrettably obscure graphic artist.

2 9

JULES CHERET
Aux Buttes Chaumont/Jouets!

1879; Chaix, Paris;
33½ x 47 in / 85 x 119.5 cm

An irresistible scene with a maternal figure representing the spirit of gift giving watching children enjoy the bounty of a department-store toy sale. Chéret executed a number of designs over the years for this store, mostly for clothing.

3 0

MISTI (FERNAND MIFLIEZ)
A La Place Clichy/Jouets Étrennes

Ca. 1895; Kossuth & Cie;
37 x 51 in / 94 x 129.5 cm

This department store advertises its toy department with the image of a beautiful young mother admiring a large marionette and arousing jealousy in the live clown at her feet. Retailers knew that mothers who came into a store on behalf of their children were also likely to make a purchase or two for themselves.

3 1

JULES CHERET
Pastilles Poncelet

1896; Chaix, Paris;
15¼ x 22 in / 38.5 x 55.8 cm

Buffeted by wind and pelted by rain, the young woman knows she can count on Poncelet cough drops to keep her in good health. Chéret was the first to understand the power of a pretty face and figure to sell. This is one of his images that proved so popular it appeared not only on full-sized posters, but was also disseminated to the public as a special insert in the periodical *Courrier Français*.

❸❸

PAUL C. HELLEU
Ed. Sagot

1900; Chaix, Paris;
29 x 41 in / 73.7 x 104.2 cm

The customer at Sagot's, one of the principal print and poster dealers in Paris, considers several pieces of artwork. Even though we see only her back, we can tell from the way she leans forward how intensely she's concentrating. Sagot was an early convert to the lure of posters and contributed substantially to the emergence of posters as collectible art in the 1890s.

❸❹

◄

JULES CHERET
Pastilles Geraudel

1896; Chaix, Paris;
34 x 38 in / 86.4 x 122 cm

Capering through a snowstorm, this blithe figure is courting a cough that Geraudel lozenges will cure. Even the bad weather can't dampen her spirits. Nothing could keep a good Chéret girl down—one of the most prominent traits of this poster pioneer.

❸❷

GEORGES DE FEURE
(GEORGES VAN SLUITERS)
Affiches et Estampes
Pierrefort

1898; Chaix, Paris;
32 x 24¹/₂ in / 81.3 x 62 cm

Is there such a thing as feminine mystique?
Georges de Feure, for one, explores that side
of the female psyche perhaps more
thoroughly than any other posterist. He views
his women as enigmatic, often portraying
them with a sly little smile of private
amusement. In this design for a print and
poster dealer the woman's strong graphic
presence and her elusive demeanor suggest
posters' powerful, often mysterious appeal.

❸❺

ALPHONSE MUCHA
F. Champenois/
Imprimeur-Editeur

1897; F. Champenois, Paris;
19 x 25¹/₂ in / 47.6 x 64.8 cm

With its universally appealing face, this Mucha design
of a woman leafing through a book eventually
appeared in special editions without text as art for
the home and became popularly known as "Reverie."
It was originally prepared by Mucha for his
printer/agent Champenois, probably as the top part
of a calendar, which is indicated by the year
designation in the upper corners. No such calendar
has been unearthed, but the design became hugely
popular with Champenois' clients and was reprinted
for a number of them with various sales messages.

❸❻

G. BERNI
Bazar de L'Hotel de Ville

1900; Pichot, Paris;
44 x 61 in / 111.8 x 154.9 cm

The pert young woman is supposed to be shopping for toys, but she is momentarily distracted by a flirtatious clown. An inspired scene to promote a turn-of-the-century toy sale.

❸ ❼

PRIVAT LIVEMONT
Michiels Frères

1902; Van Leer & Co., Amsterdam;
19³/4 x 33¹/2 in / 50.2 x 85 cm

The woman and her child admire the beauty of a garden, shown behind them in subtle earthy colors, landscaped by the nursery company named on the completed version of this poster with letters. Livemont was an ardent exponent of Art Nouveau. Here, we have a prime example of one of the movement's precepts: a reverence for women, always shown in the best possible light.

❸ ❽

►
THEOPHILE-ALEXANDRE STEINLEN
Clinique Chéron

1905; Charles Wall, Paris;
53¹/4 x 77 in / 135.2 x 195 cm

It would be hard to imagine a better design for a veterinary clinic than the pets affectionately expressing their thanks for its mothering care and concern. Steinlen was a cat lover, so the felines get top billing here.

❸ ❾

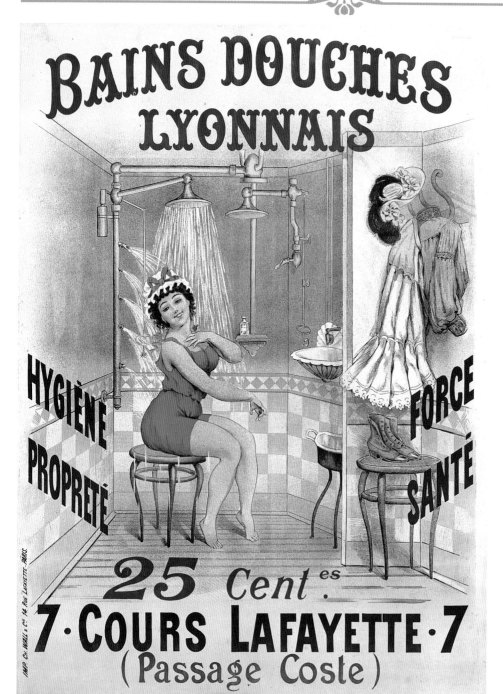

ANONYMOUS
Bains Douches
Lyonnais

Ca. 1902; Ch. Wall, Paris;
39½ × 54½ in / 100.5 × 138.5 cm

This delighted woman in skivvies and shower cap advertises a public bath house with showers. The establishment looks surprisingly well appointed, with advanced features including multiple jet streams for a full-length body massage and adjustable shower heads. "Hygiene, cleanliness, strength and health"—all for only a quarter of a franc.

❹ ⓪

Wines & Liquors

Posters for alcoholic beverages provide a good example of art leading the way to break a taboo. In the 19th century, drinking by women was regarded with scorn. Although consumption was no doubt wide, women had to conceal it as best they could. A gentleman could get away with being seen intoxicated in public now and then, but for a woman it was simply socially unacceptable. As a result, liquor ads were addressed almost exclusively to men.

Two developments led to a slow, irreversible change. In the mid-1800s, producers of stomach remedies—which then often contained bitter-tasting quinine—discovered that they could disguise the taste by lacing the medicine with alcohol. Soon various "stomach bitters" or "digestive potions" came on the market which women could openly buy and consume under the pretext that they were promoting their health.

Then came the posterists. Knowing how persuasive men find a pretty face, they put women in liquor posters and showed them not only praising the product but actually sampling it. Where straight-laced moralists portrayed drinking women as lowly sinners, posters suddenly showed respectable ladies enjoying aperitifs, champagnes, and liqueurs with gusto—alone, in the company of other women, or with a gentleman. There's no doubt that such images encouraged many a woman to break another of the period's shackles.

BARMAID OF THE 20TH CENTURY.

ANONYMOUS
Barmaid of the 20th Century

1895; Police Gazette, New York;
22¹/₂ x 16 in / 57.1 x 40.6 cm

From its small size and the fact that it was printed by a magazine publisher, this was likely an insert or supplement in *The Police Gazette*, one on the first publications to concern itself exclusively with crime stories. (Another clue is the invitation to subscribe in upper-right corner.) The poster is interesting as a historical document showing different types of customers and the high-spirited barmaid—a fixture in neighborhood saloons of the gaslight era and one way for a woman to earn a living without the drudgery of factory work.

❹❶

▶

JULES CHERET
Vin Mariani

1894; Chaix, Paris;
34 x 48¹/₂ in / 86 x 123.2 cm

One of Chéret's most uninhibited sprites, full of effervescent zest, invites us to partake of Vin Mariani, a "tonic wine," according to its maker. Made from a bordeaux base with an extract of coca leaves, it was created by Angelo Mariani, a humble young man from Corsica who came to Paris as a pharmacist's assistant. Seeing all the "stomach bitters" and "medicinal tonics" being sold, he decided to enter the market, and before long, his product had the lion's share. This may have been due to the presence of cocaine in the drink, but mostly it was a textbook case of imaginative promotional strategy. Mariani was one of the first to hit on the idea of having famous personalities and celebrities, even minor royalty, endorse his product in newspaper and magazine ads. Eventually, it paid off beyond his wildest dreams.

❹❷

PRIVAT LIVEMONT
Absinthe Robette

1896; J. Goffart, Bruxelles;
32¹/₄ x 41¹/₄ in / 83.2 x 110.5 cm

Absinthe, a potent drink made
from wormwood, was
sometimes referred to as "the
green fairy" for its color and its
hallucinogenic properties. The
artist therefore puts a green
tinge on his whole design and
evokes the intoxicating effect in
a mysterious Art-Nouveau
pattern that's half vegetable,
half vapor. The sheerly veiled
woman seems to be checking
the drink she has mixed with
an expert eye for color and
texture. An excellent example
of female sensuality used in
the service of commerce.

❹❸

▶

JULES-ALEXANDRE
GRÜN
Byrrh

1907; F. Daubenbis & Co., Paris;
47 x 62 in / 119.4 x 157.5 cm

A flamboyant figure in red
drums up business for the
aperitif Byrhh. An accepted
custom of the time was for
various alcoholic beverages to
masquerade as stomach bitters
or medicinal concoctions; this
made it socially acceptable for
women to order a drink in
public since they were doing it
for their health! Here, the
product claims to be some sort
of "hygienic tonic."

❹❹

LEONETTO CAPPIELLO
Nuyens's Menthe

1902; Vercasson, Paris;
39 x 54 in / 99 x 137.2 cm

This woman glows with good cheer as she enjoys a sip of the pink potion—she even chose her dress and accessories to match its color, possibly in celebration of the brand's centennial. This liqueur and its color are too sweet to appeal to men, but the sight of this figure unabashedly enjoying herself certainly tempted women with its spirit pleasures.

④ ⑤

JULES CHERET
Quinquina Dubonnet

1896; Chaix, Paris;
15¼ x 22½ in / 48.8 x 57.1 cm

In 1846 Paris wine agent Joseph Dubonnet decided to enter the business with a product of his own. With medicinal bitters just coming into vogue, he chose to base his drink on quinine, and to disguise its bitter taste, he mixed it with sweet wine from Greece. The result quickly gained wide acceptance; by the end of the century the company was producing three million bottles a year and exporting to many foreign countries. For this poster, Chéret worked with a live model—a charming soubrette named Lise Fleuron—and the Dubonnet family cat. The scene was so enchanting that the actress began to bill herself as "The Girl with the Dubonnet Cat," and even the cat was held over by popular demand, appearing again in another poster the following year.

④ ⑥

FRANCISCO TAMAGNO
Hysope des Alpines

Ca. 1892; La Lithographie Parisenne, Paris;
39 x 54 in / 99 x 137.2 cm

The fetching young woman holds a glass of the
advertised preparation and a sprig of the herb
used in its manufacture: hyssop, a strongly
aromatic mint found in alpine meadows and
valleys. Today her clothes seem absurd for a
mountain hike, but she is prepared for her
solo walk with binoculars and a stout stick,
and if her feet were visible, we would probably
commend her sturdy shoes.

4 7

FRANCISCO TAMAGNO
Demandez un Marra

Ca. 1905; La Lithographie Parisenne, Paris;
38½ x 55¾ in / 97.8 x 139 cm

A convivial scene in a little cafe, depicted in
fine illustrative style by a skilled designer-
lithographer. The aperitif is Quina Marra—
"quina" (sometimes "quinquina") being a
generic designation for all alcoholic beverages
containing quinine. Tamagno makes no bones
about the lustful gleam in the man's eyes, but
note who's doing the pouring. The text at the
bottom of the poster, "I drink Marra to stay
beautiful, and I drink it for my health too," is in
a southern dialect from around the region
where the aperitif is made.

4 8

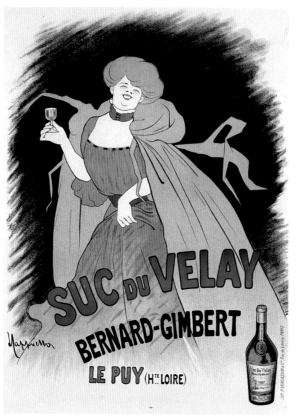

LEONETTO CAPPIELLO
Suc du Velay

1902; Vercasson, Paris;
39 x 55 in / 99 x 139.7 cm

Has a little snifter of Suc du Velay put this woman in a radiant mood, or is it that the spirit is the choice of those with a zest for life? Either way, the poster is appealing. And if the figure seems relatively tame compared to Cappiello's usual women, it's because the company wanted to present a dignified upper-class image appropriate for a premium-priced product being marketed to the gourmet trade.

4 9

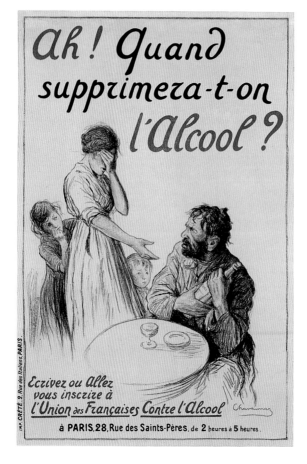

CHAVANNAZ
Ah! Quand Supprimera-t-on L'Alcool?

Ca. 1898; Imp. Crete, Paris
30⅝ x 46½ in / 120 x 183 cm

"When, oh when, will they outlaw alcohol?" cries this temperance poster, voicing the unspoken words of the wife and mother. Covering her eyes in shame — as if that would prevent her children and the rest of the world from seeing her husband's sorry state — she asks him to give up his bottle. But even if he does, it won't be for long. Drunkenness was a major social problem in France at the time, and posters promoting the Temperance Union often showed the domestic aspects of the issue. Here, Chavannaz depicts the woman as a victim; in another of his posters on the subject, he creates an allegorical scene in which the spirit of France and several of her female cohorts drive an army of bottles out of the country.

5 0

Food & Beverages

With preparation of food a traditional female prerogative, poster design had to exalt this domestic role. Showing how this task holds the family together associates the advertised product with an uplifting image. That's why posters for food products abound with doting mothers and adorable children, all enjoying life to the fullest.

Convenience products designed to cut down on kitchen drudgery for housewives and cooks were already beginning to show up at this time. A ready-made beef extract eliminated tedious hours at a hot stove; pre-whipped cream was another welcome shortcut.

Advertisers discovered the secrets of brand imagery and of surrounding their products with the trappings of elegance. Many of the posters here—with women as both their subject and audience—were so successful that versions of their images persisted for decades afterwards, and several of the brands—L-U Cookies, Chocolat Klaus, and Cacao van Houten among them—still beckon consumers today.

GEORGES MEUNIER
L'Excellent

1895; Chaix, Paris;
33¹/₂ x 48¹/₂ in / 85 x 123.2 cm

To draw our attention to this brand of beef extract
Meunier gives us one of its end uses—consommé—
served by a woman wearing an eye-popping outfit
with richly ruffled puff sleeves of the latest fashion.

❺❶

GEORGES MEUNIER
Crème Eclair

1895; Chaix, Paris;
34 x 47 in / 86.4 x 119.4 cm

Thanks to this instant whipped-cream product, this
woman escapes mess and bother. She can prepare
elegant desserts in dinner dress: cinched waist, poufy
sleeves, and flowers in her hair and decolletage—a
veritable belle of the Belle Epoque.

❺❷

▶

PRIVAT LIVEMONT
Cacao A. Driessen

1900; Van Leer & Cie, Amsterdam;
16 x 31 in / 40.6 x 78.8 cm

The serving of cocoa (this is a proof without letters;
in the version with text, the cocoa brand name
appears in the space at top) is a traditional motherly
duty, and Livemont went to great lengths to put the
point across. First of all, he gave his central figure
children as a most visible proof of motherhood; but
he also put in a chestnut tree and an elderberry to
nail it down solid: Chestnut is one of the favorite
shade trees in many Belgian and Dutch gardens under
which family gatherings are held, and elderberry,
thought to have medicinal properties, was used to
make potions which mothers gave children at the first
sign of illness. The product is being associated with
motherly care and protection, and what could be a
better recommendation? An idiosyncrasy of this artist
was a thin white outline around the woman, serving
as a sort of halo—reminiscent of the circular motifs
Mucha put behind his figures.

❺❸

PRIVAT LIVEMONT
Cacao Van Houten

1897; Van Leer & Cie, Amsterdam;
25 x 60 in / 63.5 x 152.5 cm

In Belgian artist Livemont's hands, most product posters turned into paeans to female beauty, and this is a prime example. An adherent of Art Nouveau, he used floral motifs for ornamentation: Here, for example, autumn chrysanthemums hint at how welcome a cup of cocoa would be when a chill is in the air. The woman is idealized and, like Mucha, Livemont makes free use of long flowing hair for embellishment.

🖐④

THEOPHILE-ALEXANDRE STEINLEN
Compagnie Française des Chocolats et des Thés

1895; Courmont Freres, Paris;
24½ x 32¼ in / 61.9 x 82 cm

Some of the most heart-warming poster images ever created are those in which Steinlen gives us an intimate peek into his family life. You can virtually feel his adoring love for his wife Emilie and daughter Colette, and he never fails to let us know that cats were regarded as full-fledged family members in his house. An accomplished and prolific caricaturist and illustrator, Steinlen had a concern for common people that gives his posters a deep humanism.

❺❺

►
THEOPHILE-ALEXANDRE STEINLEN
Lait Pur Stérilisé

1894; Charles Verneau, Paris;
39 x 57 in / 99 x 114.8 cm

A tranquil domestic scene that is all the more touching because it was drawn in the artist's own household and stars his young daughter. She is tasting a bowl of warmed milk before putting it down for the cats to make sure it isn't too hot for them. This endearing scene, created for an obscure rural dairy, deservedly became one of the most popular poster images of its day.

❺❻

LUCIEN LEFEVRE
Café Malt

1892; Chaix, Paris;
34 1/2 x 48 1/2 in / 87.6 x 123.2 cm

Instead of advertising properties such as aroma, flavor, and taste, this coffee brand takes a "status" approach. The image of an upper-class maid pouring a cup from an elegant silver pot implies that the product is routinely served in the best social circles. Lefèvre worked at the Chaix printing shop where Chéret was his mentor, and he acknowledges his debt to him in every design.

V. BOCCHINO
Lefèvre-Utile Biscuits

Ca. 1896; F. Champenois, Paris;
26 1/2 x 20 1/4 in / 67.3 x 51.5 cm

Among the most enlightened companies of its day, Lefèvre-Utile sought many ways to popularize its products, among them posters prepared by top artists. Here, we see an assortment of decorative boxes and toys the company used to attract youthful clientele, some of whose adorable members are obviously responding to the bait—an equally sure lure for mothers interested in pleasing their offspring.

FIRMIN BOUISSET
Chocolat Menier

1894; Camis, Paris;
36¼ x 58 in / 92 x 129.5 cm

One of the earliest instances of a single character ineradicably associated with a product was the Menier girl created by poster designer Firmin Bouisset. Originally seen from the back in an 1892 design writing the words "Chocolat Menier" on a wall, she returned many times over the years, sometimes scrawling different words in other languages, but always cutting an irresistible tomboyish figure that was instantly recognized by the public.

⑥⓪

◀

ALPHONSE MUCHA
Biscuits
Lefèvre-Utile

1896; F. Champenois, Paris;
17½ x 24¼ in / 44.5 x 61.6 cm

In one of its promotional drives in the fall of 1896, the Lefèvre-Utile company gave away 1897 calendars decorated with this ravishing design by Art-Nouveau preeminent Alphonse Mucha. Choosing a fresh young model with the facial structure and coloring of his native Moravia, Mucha gave her his trademark serpentine hair (which echoes the curlicues in the highly-wrought frame), ornamenting it with poppies and wheat of the region. He also created a pattern of wheat stalks and sickles on her dress to evoke the flour from which the biscuits are made.

⑤⑨

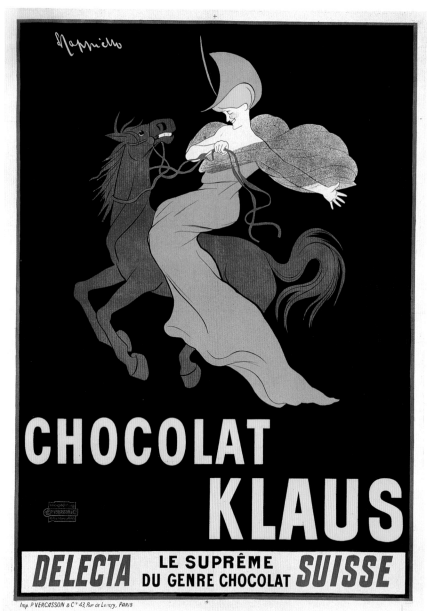

LEONETTO CAPPIELLO
Chocolat Klaus

1903; Vercasson, Paris;
46¹/₂ x 63 in / 118.5 x 160 cm

In Cappiello we find the prototype of
the modern advertising designer,
sweeping out the cobwebs of the past
century and striking out in wholly new
directions. He is, in every way, the
antithesis of Mucha. Where the older
artist understated, Cappiello overstates.
Where painstaking craftsmanship was
Mucha's motto, a few bold strokes is all
that Cappiello needs. Where Mucha
carefully differentiated between delicate
pastel hues, Cappiello works with flat
planes of strong colors, often against a
stark black background. Here, he also
attracts our attention with an
outrageous incongruity. What
connection could there be between a
lady in green on a red horse and the
chocolate she is supposed to advertise?
But we are captivated by the powerful
image, and our mind connects it with
the product in spite of ourselves. We
will never know if Cappiello set out
deliberately to create such a far-fetched
product association; most likely it came
to him intuitively. Be that as it may, he
knew a good thing when he saw it; the
effectiveness of the concept was
demonstrated, and the advertising
community sat up and took notice.

6 1

▶

EMILE G. GIRAN
Grande Patisserie
Lisboa

Ca. 1896; Sicard & Farradesche, Paris;
38¹/₂ x 57¹/₂ in / 97.8 x 146 cm

The opening of a pastry shop is
announced by the picture of a pretty
pastry chef hard at work, inspired by a
winged spirit rising from her flambé pan.
Bottles of port and madeira indicate that
every effort will be made to create the
most refined treats possible.

6 2

ALPHONSE MUCHA
Flirt

1899; F. Champenois, Paris;
12¹/₂ x 25¹/₂ in / 31.2 x 64.8 cm

To bring home the name of the product, Mucha created a discreet flirtation which embodies the 19th-century ideal of a romantic encounter: the girl demure and coy, the gentleman gently persuasive, the setting a fragrant garden. But he didn't forget the sponsor: The wrought-iron gate carries the name, and the girl's dress features a print pattern of the letters L-U, a subtle decorative reminder.

⑥❸

ALBERT A. GUILLAUME
Biscuits Pernot/Genève

1899; Cami, Paris;
14¹/₄ x 20¹/₂ in / 35.9 x 52 cm

The attractive young woman, fashionably dressed in leg-o'-mutton sleeves, brings our attention to a brand of cookies. A standard approach executed by a skilled caricaturist and illustrator with offhand ease.

⑥❹

ADRIEN BARRERE
Pêcheurs Réunis

Ca. 1907; Imp. 22 rue Philippe de Girard, Paris;
43¹/₂ x 57¹/₂ in / 110.5 x 146 cm

The association of food products with a nurturing female figure is a venerable advertising ploy. Leave it to caricaturist Adrien Barrère to give the technique an edge with fishwife "Mother Angot" who sings the praises of seafood from the United Fisheries. She may seem a little coarse, but she knows her business.

⑥❺

Bicycles & Cars

The invention of the bicycle gave women a whole degree of freedom they had never experienced before. From medieval times, the average woman rarely ventured more than a short walk away from her house, her church, and the market in her lifetime. If there were any excursions, they usually involved entire extended families, and trips by coaches or trains inevitably meant chaperones and companions.

The bicycle made the first real break in this; in a few minutes a woman could now get miles away from her house all by herself and experience the thrill of independent motion. The bicycle changed social customs, gave women self-confidence, even influenced fashion: Since pedaling in traditional clothes was an impossibly awkward task, lighter and more convenient clothing had to be developed. Far more than a means of simple transportation, the bicycle became, for women, a veritable symbol of unprecedented freedom.

Poster designers of the time sensed this. Many bicycle posters which today seem excessively flamboyant were, in the light of their times, effective symbolic expressions of the bicycle's emancipating power. A similar milestone was reached later when automobiles came on the market and allowed women to move further along the road to equality.

PAL (JEAN DE PALEOLOGUE)
Société la Française

Ca. 1894; Paul Dupont, Paris;
34¹/₂ x 48 in / 87.6 x 121.9 cm

With the name of the product already saying, in effect, "Frenchie," Pal makes doubly sure that its embodiment exudes an unmistakable French flavor. Wearing the national colors and a jaunty beret, the shapely sylph glides through the air with the greatest of ease. Anyone failing to heed the sales pitch is obviously an unpatriotic traitor.

❻❻

PAL (JEAN DE PALEOLOGUE)
Fernand Clément & Cie

1895; Paul Dupont, Paris;
42¹/₂ x 58¹/₂ in / 107.3 x 148.6 cm

The voluptuous beauty in ecstasy expresses the feeling of unrestrained freedom which the bicycle could bring into a 19th-century woman's life. Now able to cover distances under their own power, women felt there was a whole new frontier opening to them, as indeed there was. Pal gives this euphoria palpable substance.

❻❽

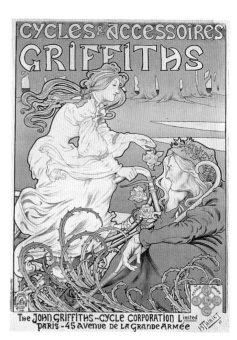

HENRI THIRIET
Cycles & Accessoires Griffiths

Ca. 1898; J. Barreau, Paris;
36¹/₄ x 50¹/₄ in / 92.1 x 127.6 cm

With effortless grace she glides along on her Griffiths bike, her voluminous dress and long hair rippling in the breeze. As was the case with most Art-Nouveau designers, Thiriet lets the woman's joy of riding express the advantages of the advertised brand without attempting to get to the technical side of the subject at all. An embodiment of old age—"Mother" Time—looks on, perhaps disapproving, perhaps envying the new speed and freedom of the age.

❻❼

H. GRAY (HENRI BOULANGER)
Cycles Sirius

1899; Courmont Freres, Paris;
38¹/₂ x 54¹/₂ in / 97.8 x 107.8 cm

If any artist could rival Pal when it came to exploiting female anatomy in posters, it was multi-talented Gray. A graphic journeyman who drew caricatures, supplied illustrations, and executed all types of design, he could readily adapt his style to the requirements of different clients with startlingly impressive results. Here, probably (if unconsciously) somewhat under Pal's influence, he creates an unabashed rider soaring on her cycle to its namesake—the brightest star in the heavens.

6 9

▶

MANUEL ROBBE
Plasson Cycles

1895; Bourgerie & Cie, Paris;
33¹/₂ x 47 in / 85.1 x 119.4 cm

In 1851 Amelia Bloomer took a step toward emancipation by appearing in public in loose pants gathered at the knee—the first sensible costume for some of the sports and athletics in which women were now hesitantly taking part. The term "bloomers" came into the language at this time, and as we can see here, they were ideally suited to biking. The young woman is still not completely confident, and the gallant gentleman is carefully guiding her.

7 0

G. BRISSARD
Cycles Mentor

Ca. 1895; printer not shown;
12¼ x 18½ in / 31.2 x 47 cm

The cycling pair seems to be having a good time: They've suspended lanterns from their handlebars so they can pedal away safely and enjoyably at night. From the small size of this design, it was likely meant to be used for point-of-purchase window display.

7 1

FRANCISCO TAMAGNO
Cycles Automoto

Ca. 1898; printer not shown;
14½ x 22½ in / 37.2 x 57.5 cm

The manufacturer wanted to boast about his factory, and the posterist thought it would be better to show a pretty young woman on a cycling excursion; this design is the happy compromise. If the cyclist is a fantasy, so is the factory: It's unlikely that the Automoto cycle shop was quite the industrial giant depicted.

7 2

▶

H. GRAY & CHARLES BRUN
Cycles Buffalo

Ca. 1902; Courmont Freres, Paris;
39 x 54¼ in / 99 x 137.8 cm

To capitalize on the cycle's name, the designers came up with a highly original concept: a buffalo being run down by a bike, ridden by no less than a pistol-packing woman. Actually, the idea of a female gunslinger wasn't that far-fetched. In 1902, Buffalo Bill's Wild West show made a tour of Europe, and the French, who held romanticized views of the American West, fell for it lock, stock and Annie Oakley.

7 3

ALPHONSE MUCHA
Waverly Cycles

1898; F. Champenois, Paris;
43 × 33½ in / 109.2 × 85 cm

Manufactured in Indianapolis, the Waverly was also marketed aggressively overseas. The maker's claim for the machine was its sturdy construction; Mucha does not attempt to show any technical details, but instead personifies the strong steel frame with a beautiful woman leaning on an anvil, dressed (although barely) in a blacksmith's leather apron. She holds a laurel branch symbolizing the prizes won by the bicycle in various competitions and exhibitions. The bicycle is hardly visible; Mucha expects the woman and her gaze of utter assurance to do the convincing.

❼❹

E. THELEM
(ERNEST BARTHELEMY LEM)
Cycles Peugot

Ca. 1897; Edw. Ancourt, Paris;
42 × 58 in / 106 × 146.7 cm

The young dandy assumes a calculatedly casual posture against his new Peugeot motorbike to observe a women's lawn tennis game, and one of the players approaches for a closer look. One must admire the women for playing in their confining clothes. Ironically, the Peugeot family made its fortune manufacturing corsets before it turned to cycles in 1885.

❼❺

MARCELLIN AUZOLLE
Auto Barré

Ca. 1903; Th. Dupuy & Fils, Paris;
59 x 44 in / 150 x 111.7 cm

The two women have just passed a string of other
automobiles, and one of them can't resist bragging about their
vehicle's superiority with a sassy, surprising thumbing of her
nose. The poster not only implies that women should take up
motoring, but also shows how the freedom of the road may
lead them to break some of the shackles of the era's propriety.
It's hard to tell what astounds the gathered villagers most: the
women's beauty, their nerve, or their ramshackle contraption.
An altogether delightful time capsule by a highly competent but
unfortunately obscure poster master.

7 8

PRIVAT LIVEMONT
Automobile Club de France

1903; F. Champenois, Paris;
38 x 51 in / 96.2 x 129.5 cm

In 1902 and 1903 Livemont created several posters for the Automobile Club of France and its shows, personifying the organization with his delicate Art-Nouveau women. Here, the figure is seated on a throne in front of the Grand Palais exhibition hall, drenched in roses and surrounded by hints of an international throng come to admire progress. As was Livemont's custom, he gives the auto goddess a white outline, this time adding a halo resembling an automotive flywheel.

7 7

EUGENE GRASSET
Marque Georges Richard

1899; G. de Malherbe, Paris;
59 x 42½ in / 149.2 x 198 cm

A characteristic specimen of image advertising. Of the product, we see barely a handlebar; it is the moody and enigmatic rider who carries the weight of the sale. Georges Richard was one of quite a number of bicycle manufacturers who were hurriedly adding automobiles as a sideline around the turn of the century; within a few years, the sideline would become the main or, as here, the only product of the company.

7 8

Publications

One of the biggest social changes of the 19th century was urbanization, a result of the expansion of industry and the subsequent availability of jobs in cities. With more money and leisure time available than agrarian settings afforded, urban populations avidly reached out for intellectual and spiritual experiences. Now better educated, people acquired an appreciation of culture, art, and literature. As the posters for reading matter attest, there was a hunger for books and magazines that brought the outside world to the reader as never before.

The traditional epic and romantic literature of the past was being supplemented by a more realistic view of life. Subjects formerly considered blasphemous, evil, or merely impolite were brought out into the open. There were books about families breaking down, alcoholism, prostitution, even incest.

This was, in fact, the golden era of popular reading. With no movies, radio, or television, reading was not only entertainment, but the best window to the world, and there were more newspapers, magazines, and books published than at any other time in history.

Reading benefited women more than men in this period: While the percentage of women in the work force was beginning to grow—in 1900 18% of the available jobs were filled by women—women still generally had more leisure hours at home than men and thus read more. Much of the awareness of important social issues which eventually led to the feminist movement can no doubt be traced to women's increasing interest in reading.

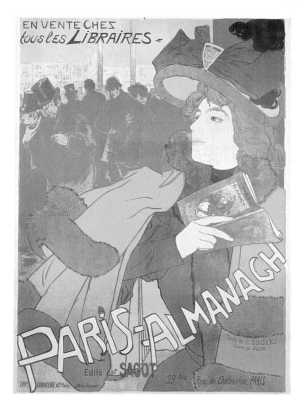

GEORGES DE FEURE
(GEORGES VAN SLUITERS)
Paris-Almanach

1894; Bourgerie & Cie., Paris;
23¹/₂ x 31 in / 59.6 x 78.7 cm

The advertised booklet was a guide to Paris attractions published by Ed. Sagot, which de Feure shows in the hand of a woman traveling alone and wishing to sample the pulse of the city. As always, the artist manages to suggest hidden depths. Although looking at the merry throng, the figure remains a bit apart, oddly aloof, and slightly mysterious.
7 9

ETHEL REED
Miss Träumerei

1895; Lamson & Wolfe, Boston
13³/₄ x 22 in / 35 x 55.9 cm

Ethel Reed's designs always have an air of genteel refinement, with images of tender compassion and sentiment. She was thus the logical choice to advertise a novel whose heroine personifies Schumann's celebrated romantic piano composition "Träumerei" ("Dreaming"), which the author borrowed for the title. Like virtually every profession at the time, poster design was a male preserve; that Ethel Reed could rise to become an acknowledged leader among American posterists of the period is a tribute to her artistic superiority and impeccable taste. What a loss that after marrying, she disappeared completely from the poster field.
8 0

►

JULES CHERET
Physique & Chimie Populaires

1885; Chaix, Paris;
34¹/₄ x 48¹/₂ in / 87 x 122.5 cm

This was a library of popular science being offered to the public in 10-centime installments; Chéret, of course, could not resist picturing an attractive young student poring over a science text. The idea of a woman in the still very masculine world of science was daring; when Marie Curie worked on radioactivity in the late 1890s, she was one of a mere handful of women who had the temerity to defy preconceived notions of their proper place in society.
8 1

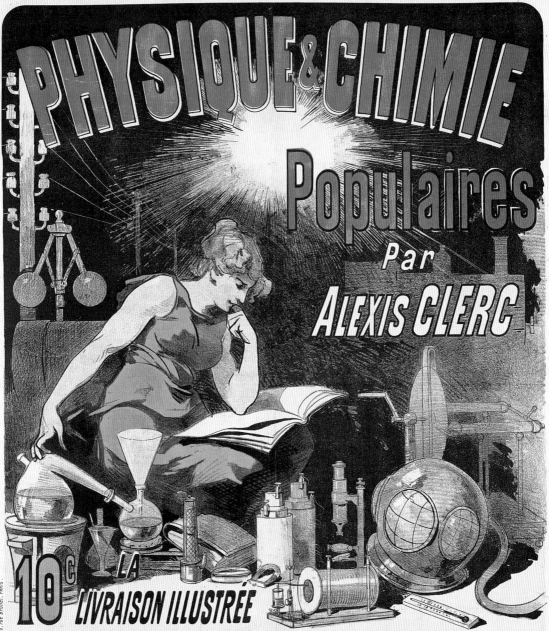

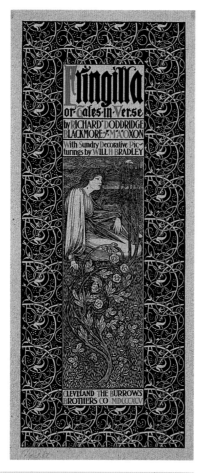

WILL H. BRADLEY
Fringilla

1895; Wayside Press, Springfield, Mass.;
10 x 21 in / 25.2 x 52.7 cm

As can be seen in all of Bradley's work, he was fascinated with ornamental patterns, using them to frame and permeate every image, incorporating naturally decorative elements like flowers, and working out each curlicue with exceedingly fine care. Here, he advertises a volume of poetry by depicting a languid young woman communing with nature.

8 2

LUCIEN FAURE
Claudine

1901; Charle Verneau, Paris;
39¹/₂ x 55 in / 100.5 x 139.6 cm

Two books about Claudine, a popular schoolgirl literary heroine around the turn of century, are offered for five-and-a-half francs each. (Their authorship here is attributed to the newspaperman and playwright Willy, who, in fact, stole the credit from his wife Colette). Faure chose to advertise them by depicting the dynamic and controversial performer Polaire, who played the role on stage. Endowed with a generous bosom, the actress defied convention from the start of her career in her mid-teens by refusing to confine her figure in the corsets prescribed by fashion dictates of the day. Both on stage and in private she appeared in clothes that made no attempt to conceal, predictably pushing her career ever higher.

8 3

►

EUGENE GRASSET
Librairie Romantique

1887; J. Bognard, Paris;
37 x 50 in / 94 x 127 cm

The publisher Ed. Monnier & Cie. came out with a series of romantic novels for which Grasset prepared this memorable image that eloquently summarizes the age of romanticism: a young woman in velvet and lace, deeply absorbed in an imaginary adventure which she will probably never experience in her confined real life. Even with her back turned to us, her yearnings are clearly expressed. Grasset treats his subject with utmost discretion, yet manages to let us in on her suppressed longings. The poster was used for the entire series, with names of individual volumes changed appropriately in the text area.

8 4

Ed. MONNIER et Cᵉ, Editeurs

EN VENTE CHEZ TOUS LES LIBRAIRES

L'AGE
DU
ROMANTISME

Splendide publication in-4°, illustrée
PARAISSANT PAR LIVRAISONS DE 12 PAGES

**Prosateurs, Poètes, Orateurs, Musiciens
Peintres, Graveurs, Aquafortistes, etc.**

NOMBREUSES ILLUSTRATIONS DANS LE TEXTE & HORS TEXTE

REPRODUISANT DES DOCUMENTS INÉDITS OU RARISSIMES DE LA PÉRIODE ROMANTIQUE

Sous la direction de MM. Ph. BURTY et Maurice TOURNEUX

PRINCIPAUX COLLABORATEURS :

Tʜ. ᴅᴇ BANVILLE — BERGERAT — CHAMPFLEURY — CHESNEAU — CLARETIE
DARCEL — A. DUMAS — A. DUSOLLIER — Eᴍ. ᴅᴇꜱ ESSARTS — GÉDALGER
G. ISAMBERT — JULIEN — Dᴇ LOVENJOUL — P. MANTZ — C. MENDÈS — P. MEURICE
Cʜ. MONSELET — Dᴇ ʟᴀ POMMERAYE — G. POUCHET — M. PROTH — L. ULBACH
SPULLER — Aᴜɢ. VACQUERIE, ᴇᴛᴄ., ᴇᴛᴄ.

Corbell — Chromotyp. Crété.

J. BOGNARD Jᴹᴱ 28, Bᵈ DE LA CONTRESCARPE, PARIS

HENRI DE TOULOUSE-LAUTREC
Elles

1896; printer not shown;
17¼ x 22¼ in / 45.1 x 57.8 cm

Elles ("They") was a portfolio of ten lithographs by Toulouse-Lautrec of a Paris house of prostitution; this design was used on the cover, as frontispiece, and also, with text added, as a poster for the published volume. Toulouse-Lautrec's sketches show the prostitutes not involved with clients, but at their daily personal routines: grooming, tidying their rooms, resting, or amusing themselves. It was his way, as an artist, of making a statement for tolerance: These women, he seemed to say, are only human beings, doing and enjoying many of the same things everybody does, so why condemn them? Note the sensitive way he suggests the woman's trade without being either coy or blatant: Just a man's hat on top of her underthings states the case with detached neutrality.

❽❺

►

THEOPHILE-ALEXANDRE STEINLEN
L'Assommoir

1900; Charles Verneau, Paris;
54¾ x 93½ in / 136.5 x 237.5 cm

L'Assommoir ("The Gin Mill") was Emile Zola's first novel and one of his realistic works which pioneered a new trend in literature, discarding the flowery lyricism of the romantic age in favor of a hard look at the problems of common people. Steinlen, whose empathy for the working class matches Zola's, portrays the protagonist couple whose life is eventually destroyed by alcohol without flattery but with compassion. The pair of ordinary lovers out for a little drink are not yet aware that the place where they are sitting will become the decisive factor in their pitiful existence. The poster is for a play based on the novel.

❽❻

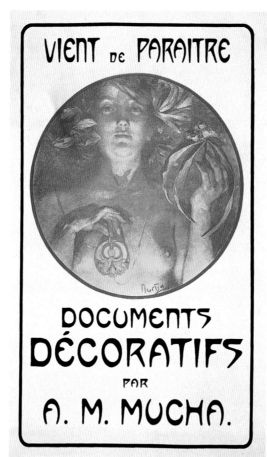

ALPHONSE MUCHA
Documents Décoratifs

1901; F. Champenois, Paris;
18 x 30 in / 45 x 75.5 cm

Mucha publicizes his own book, a text on Art Nouveau style elements which art schools throughout the world continued to use until the style itself went out of fashion. Not surprisingly, the author chooses a woman in an allegorical pose—his favorite method of artistic expression. It is woman as an embodiment of all that is pure and beautiful, the unattainable ideal that Mucha aspired to capture with earnest ardor in nearly all his poster designs. The book contained many examples of ways to pose and portray women along with various types of ornamental borders, framing devices, and other techniques to achieve compositional harmony and produce memorable images.

8 7

ALPHONSE MUCHA
L'Estampe Moderne

1897; F. Champenois, Paris;
23 x 31½ in / 58 x 79.7 cm

This was a collector's edition of 100 color lithographs from the best contemporary artists, appearing in monthly issues of four prints each, between May 1897 and April 1899. Nearly all of the designs were commissioned for this project exclusively; Mucha himself contributed two of them (*Salome* and *Salammbo*) and also designed this narrow panel which appeared on all the covers. With a few spare strokes, he works his magic: classic face, flowing hair, a lithographer's crayon, and voilà! Another idealized Mucha beauty. Interestingly, even a minor Mucha work like this intrigued the artist's champion and good client Sarah Bernhardt. She had it printed in New York in 1905 (with a few embellishing touches by another artist) to announce her American tour that year.

8 8

PIERRE BONNARD
L'Estampe et L'Affiche

1897; printer not shown;
23¹/₄ x 31³/₄ in / 59 x 80.6 cm

The bi-weekly magazine *L'Estampe et L'Affiche* was a pioneering proponent of collecting posters as well as traditional prints, and its influence was no doubt partly responsible for the poster craze of the last half of the 1890s. Bonnard, a highly talented graphic artist, expressed the whole phenomenon with this design: The old lady putting on her glasses stands for the older Print who wants to get a good look at the brash young Poster running around with a portfolio full of drawings and sketches— the new generation clamoring for recognition. In addition to advertising the publication on the streets of Paris, this design also appeared in the first issue of March 1897.

⑧⑨

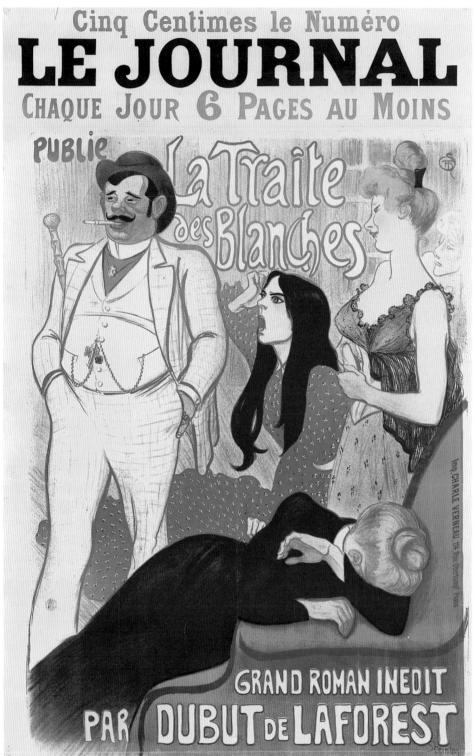

THEOPHILE-ALEXANDRE STEINLEN
Le Journal/ La Traite des Blanches

1899; Charle Verneau, Paris;
48¹/₄ x 74 in / 122.5 x 188 cm

Quite a few literary works in this era first saw the light of day as installments printed in daily or weekly papers; the reason was competition among papers, as they tried to induce readers to become permanent subscribers. A major novel appearing in a trickle would hold readers for several months, with the hope that they would get used to the paper's other features and remain loyal afterwards. The lure of a new sensational novel was often used to advertise the paper itself. And sensational is the word for this Steinlen poster advertising installments of "White Slavery." It depicts a heartless pimp with three of his victims. One is arguing passionately for her freedom, one seems resigned to her fate, and one is in utter despair. In Steinlen's original version, the willing prostitute had her breasts bared, but there was an adverse reaction to the poster, and this censored version was hastily substituted.

90

ANONYMOUS
L'Inceste

Ca. 1897; H. Laas, Paris;
31 x 43 in / 78 x 109.5 cm

The problem of incest is as old
as mankind, but there always
existed a reluctance to tackle
the subject openly; yet here we
have a novel that not only deals
with it but blatantly announces
it right in its title. The breaking
of many social taboos like this
was one of the major trends in
public life as the 19th century
gave way to the 20th. The
illustration in this poster
graphically depicts the tragic
consequences of the great sin.
The novel is being sold on the
installment plan at 10 centimes
per issue; this was a common
practice at the time to achieve
wider circulation for books, the
idea being that many people
who might be too poor or
simply unwilling to part with
two or three francs for a whole
unknown book could be lured
to read the first few pages for
10 centimes and become
hooked to buy the remaining
sections in weekly doses. As
the last installment went to
press, there was an additional
opportunity for profit for the
publishers: They offered to
provide, for an extra fee, a
handsome cover, which the
customer could take to any
bookbinder with all the
installments and have them
bound into a regular
hardcover book.

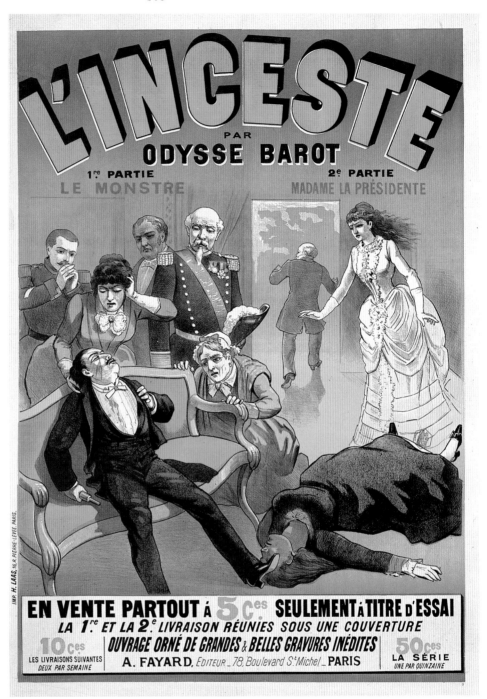

HENRI DE TOULOUSE-LAUTREC
La Revue Blanche

1895; Edw. Ancourt, Paris;
36¹/₄ x 50 in / 92 x 127 cm

With letters added, this design advertised
the fortnightly *La Revue Blanche*, an avant-
garde artistic and literary periodical that was
founded in Belgium in 1889 by the Natanson
brothers and moved to Paris when they did.
There, they were among the first to
recognize Toulouse-Lautrec's unconventional
genius, and they freely published his drawings
in the magazine. They also became friends
socially, and the artist became a frequent
participant in intimate gatherings at the home
of one of the brothers, Thadée Natanson,
whose wife Misia enjoyed the company of
stimulating intellectuals, artists, and writers.
It is Misia we see in this poster, and her
rather unusual stance is explained by the fact
that it is actually a portrait of her on skates.
As one of the movers and shakers among the
literary set, Misia was one of the most
emancipated women of her generation.
Toulouse-Lautrec, who could be mercilessly
scathing, pays her homage with an entirely
sympathetic portrayal. This version of the
poster without text was issued in a limited
edition of 50.

92

►

PAUL BALLURIAU
L'Eclair

Ca. 1896; Delattre & Juliot, Paris;
23 x 31 in/ 58.4 x 75.8 cm

L'Eclair was an independent, politically
oriented journal which devoted a lot of
effort to advertising by means of posters and,
in fact, held one of the most hotly contested
competitions for the best poster of the year.
Balluriau was primarily a book illustrator;
here, he offers an allegorical vision of France
looking toward a new dawn. In the
background, however, the figure fills the
completely modern role of a newspaper
clerk taking down messages from an early
telegraph machine.

93

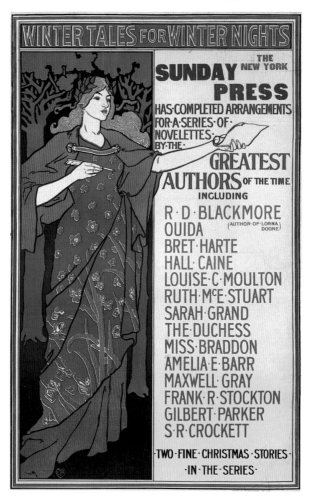

LOUIS RHEAD
Winter Tales for Winter Nights/Sunday Press

1896; Ellery Howard Co., New York;
29 x 46¹/₂ in / 73.6 x 118.1 cm

A collection of short fiction published by *The New York Sunday Press* is offered by a redhead in an unusual print dress. Rhead, a versatile designer who favored Art Nouveau style, could be counted on to give any poster a decorative flair; the dress design is quite likely his own creation.

9 4

ANONYMOUS
The Delineator

1892; printer not shown;
17 x 12¹/₂ in / 43.2 x 31.8 cm

This rare, very fine design for an obscure American fashion magazine shows that high-quality work was being done in the U.S. at the same time that Paris and London were considered the world capitals of poster art. It was mainly due to lack of American interest in poster acquisition as a hobby that so many of these minor gems were lost to posterity.

9 5

LEONETTO CAPPIELLO
Le Journal

1900; Charle Verneau, Paris;
11½ x 14½ in / 29.5 x 36.8 cm

This is one of Cappiello's early poster works, its small size suggesting that it's actually more of a point-of-purchase flier. In the caricaturistic style that reflects his previous career, Cappiello shows a *Le Journal* reader who is clearly as "literary" and "well-informed" as the paper itself.

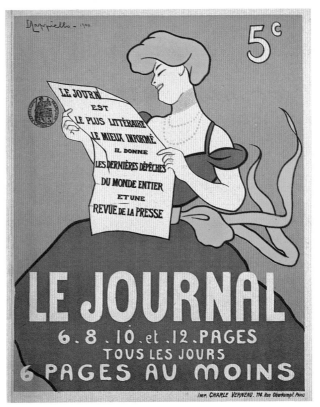

ALPHONSE MUCHA
Zodiac/La Plume

1896; F. Champenois, Paris;
19 x 25¾ in / 48.2 x 65.5 cm

This image, originally a calendar for the Champenois printing firm, became one of Mucha's most popular and durable creations. At least a dozen commercial uses have been uncovered, for diverse clients in several cities, and many others probably remain unknown to us. The artist used all his skills to illustrate his enchantment with feminine adornment: meandering hair, elaborate dress, jeweled headwear—and the fact that the project was a calendar enabled him to use the zodiac as a fantastic halo to frame the profile. There is something serene, profound, and captivating about this face that gave this design a longevity that even the artist himself couldn't have anticipated. This particular version, apparently the second use of the work, incorporated a calendar advertising the magazine *La Plume,* whose editor, Leon Deschamps, was one of Mucha's most active supporters.

CLEMENTINE-HELENE DUFAU
La Fronde

1898; Charle Verneau, Paris;
54¹/₂ x 39 in / 138.4 x 99 cm

La Fronde was the organ of the French radical feminist movement
founded by suffragette Marguerite Durand. The magazine aroused
much controversy, and local ordinances were passed forbidding its
dissemination in schools and workplaces, or sale on newsstands.
Despite this persecution, the periodical somehow survived until
World War I. In the design, the woman in green obviously stands for
Durand, symbolically pointing the way forward to her followers. The
artist Dufau was an outspoken champion of women's rights herself,
and this poster justly became her most famous work.

9 8

▶

THEOPHILE-ALEXANDRE
STEINLEN
Le Petit Sou

1900; Charle Verneau, Paris;
39¹/₄ x 65 in / 96 x 159 cm

Representing the French Republic, an allegorical
Marianne breaks her shackles and leads her people
in an attack on the aristocracy and church in this
poster for a Socialist periodical. Steinlen often
joined various left-wing causes, expressing his
conviction in compellingly eloquent designs; this
one is exceptionally powerful.

9 9

EDWARD PENFIELD
Poster Calendar 1897

1896; Harper's, New York;
10¼ x 18 in / 26 x 45.7 cm

This calendar consists of five sheets: a cover which features the artist's self-portrait at work, observed by his cat, and four seasonal designs with three months on each. It's pure Penfield: a simple, clear-cut design in flat colors showing upper-crust people engaged in interesting pursuits. It's also an expression of *Harper's* as a magazine for people who strive for elegance and sophistication. Such an improvement in social status, it was subtly implied, could be achieved at least partly by judicious perusal of the ambitious monthly.

100

EDWARD PENFIELD
Harper's/May

1896; Harper's, New York;
12 x 18 in / 30.5 x 45.7 cm

During his tenure as art director for *Harper's* (1893-99), Penfield created a new poster for every month's issue, yet never seemed to run out of fresh ideas. This is one of his most inspired. The woman holds two obviously pampered cats who rejoice at the attention; the woman, however, appears almost disconcerted, not quite sure where—or if—to put them down. The image has an extraordinary domestic charm and remains one of the most highly sought among collectors of American poster art.

101

EDWARD PENFIELD
Harper's/September

1896; Harper's, New York;
18¼ x 13¾ in / 46.3 x 34.9 cm

No one surpassed the fruitful collaboration between *Harper's* and the magazine's house artist Penfield in sheer longevity: For some ten years, he produced a string of monthly promotional placards for the publication, always managing to come up with a fresh idea for each and every issue. His drawings look deceptively simple yet they always make the point that elegant people of style read the publication. *Harper's* wanted to attract young trend-setters as readers, and Penfield always gave them something visual to identify with or aspire to.

❶⓪❷

WILL CARQUEVILLE
Lippincott's/April

1895; Will Carqueville, Chicago;
12½ x 19 in / 31.7 x 48.2 cm

The 1890s were the heyday of small magazines, most of them slanting their stories and articles to attract women readers. Pre-radio and television, many women had no recreation other than reading, and while classic books were educational requirements, contemporary magazines provided a glimpse of the current scene they couldn't obtain otherwise. *Lippincott's*, based in Philadephia, was one such monthly, and the poster shows a trio of avid readers perusing the issue for April 1895. At this time these in-store placards announcing each month's issue were customarily produced by either house artists or permanently-engaged outside contractors. In this case, it was Chicago-based Will Carqueville who supplied *Lippincott's* for several years; he was succeeded by J.J. Gould.

❶⓪❸

LOUIS RHEAD
Scribner's/for Xmas

1895; Louis Rhead, New York;
13½ x 19½ in / 35 x 49.5 cm

A red-haired beauty brings some Christmas greenery to her house through a snowy wood in this charming design for *Scribner's*, one of the most popular magazines of its kind. Even by Rhead's own high standards, this is a classic.

❶⓪❹

WILL H. BRADLEY
The Chap-Book/
Being a Miscellany

1895; Will H. Bradley;
14 x 21 1/2 in / 35.6 x 54.6 cm

In 1894 two Harvard students, Herbert Stone and Ingalls Kimball, came up with an idea for a magazine called *The Chap Book* that would cover literary and artistic news not normally covered in major journals—including the notion of regarding posters as an art form. Although it was not intended to be anything more than a bit of college high-jinks, the tiny curiosity (5.5 x 8 inches in size) surprised the two by prospering and became enough of a hit that when they returned to their native Chicago, they continued to publish it there for some years. Bradley contributed to the success of the original issues of *The Chap Book* with store-counter placards such as this one and created a total of five designs for the publication; this is the only one in black and white.

The influence of Art Nouveau, and especially its British exponent Aubrey Beardsley, is clearly apparent, and the tender, romantic image piques our interest in the "curious and interesting songs, ballads, tales, histories etc." promised in the text below.

❶❶❺

WILL H. BRADLEY
Bradley/His Book/June

1896; Will H. Bradley;
8 5/8 x 19 3/4 in / 22 x 50.2 cm

One of the earliest American converts to Art Nouveau, this maverick printer/publisher/designer produced a number of posters of surpassing beauty and meticulous craftsmanship. Here, he uses what has been dubbed his "Queen of Hearts" design to announce the upcoming June 1896 issue of his own small magazine. He started publishing in late 1895 when he opened his own printing establishment, the Wayside Press, in Springfield, Massachusetts.

❶❶❻

ANONYMOUS
Harper's/June/Thackeray

1911; Harper's, New York;
21 × 11 in / 53.5 × 28 cm

Two daintily portrayed young ladies invite us to buy the June 1911 issue of *Harper's*, which boast of its longevity in the magazine field. This promotional placard for a single issue of a magazine is one of the last of its breed; point-of-sale advertising was giving way to more mass-oriented approaches: outdoor posters and print media.

❶⓪❼

PAL (JEAN DE PALEOLOGUE)
Truth for April

1901; Truth Publishing, New York;
13¹⁄₂ × 26¹⁄₂ in / 34.3 × 67.3 cm

A sophisticated fashion plate alerts potential readers to the fact that *Truth* is paying attention to high-society doings and the latest trends in stylish attire. Although Pal gave up his preoccupation with near-nude sirens once he left Paris for America, he continued to prove that the female form was his unchallenged specialty.

❶⓪❽

►

VÁCLAV OLIVA
Zlatá Praha

Ca. 1898; J. Otty, Praha;
15¹⁄₂ × 42¹⁄₂ in / 39.3 × 107.9 cm

Zlatá Praha ("Golden Prague") was a richly illustrated Czech weekly with a mixture of entertaining and enlightening stories on many subjects. A pioneer in marketing techniques, it kept readers' interests alive with special inserts, premiums, and contests. The woman nonchalantly tucking an issue under her arm looks more like a Paris fashion model than a citizen of this small middle-European country, making it clear that Prague lived on the cutting edge of world fashions.

❶⓪❾

PAL (JEAN DE PALEOLOGUE)
Truth for July

1901; Truth Publishing, New York;
13 x 28¼ in / 33 x 71.7 cm

Truth, a lively, enterprising magazine, was
one of the first American clients for Pal
when, after having made a name for
himself in Paris with his delectable poster
temptresses, he decided to move to the
U.S. in 1900. *Truth* appeared in New York
in 1881 as a weekly at 10¢ an issue; in 1899
it switched to a monthly format at 25¢
and made a determined grab for the
all-important women readers by putting
emphasis on fashion and art. Pal expresses
the magazine's new orientation eloquently
with a cluster of seasonal poppies and the
face of what he hoped was a typical reader.

🄸🄸🄸

ANONYMOUS
Le Petit Parisien

1908; Le Petit Parisien, Paris;
9½ x 12 in / 24.1 x 30.5 cm.

Le Petit Parisien was known for its tireless promotion of sporting competitions, especially in provincial cities where a race sponsored by a Paris paper became a major event. There were bicycle and motorcycle races, automobile rallies, even balloon-flying contests; here, with aviation only five years old, the newspaper is distributing calendars showing a woman piloting a plane. Particularly daring given that at this time there was no famous aviatrix who had made a name for herself in popular imagination; Amelia Earhart would not come on the scene until a quarter-century later.

❶ ❶ ❶

MOSNAR YENDIS
(SIDNEY RANSOM)
The Poster

1898; David Allen & Sons, London;
19½ x 30 in / 49.5 x 76 cm.

To advertise a magazine that covered the poster scene in England, little-known artist Sidney Ransom (who habitually signed his name backwards) came up with a whimsical design in which a poster man steps out of his drawing to admire a poster woman on another design. An instructive example of how to deal effectively with the subject of posters, this remains the most admired legacy of an artist who was probably a caricaturist—most of his preserved work falls into that category.

❶ ❶ ❷

Apparel

If there is one word that defines the 19th-century attitude to clothing, it's "overdress." Layers upon layers of underwear, slips, petticoats, and outerwear were piled upon the female body, summer and winter, indoors and out, so that hardly an inch of skin would show. (Even the most scandalous invention of the Belle Epoque, the cancan, didn't escape this skin phobia: We don't really see the dancers' naked flesh, just frilly pantaloons and stockings.) At the beach, those few who actually went into the water (and that was decidedly a minority) put on outfits that covered them from neck to knee.

The idea that a woman could not appear in public without subjecting herself to the torture of the corset was one of the most rigidly ingrained concepts of the 19th century. Not until the 1880s did the world even dare to consider that it might actually survive seeing a woman without the confining garment; this was mainly due to women's taking up horse riding, bicycling, and sports like tennis which required more freedom of movement than the tightly-laced corset allowed. Of course the corset was still very much around, as the posters for foundation garments attest; but, in fact, the posters themselves, revealing to the general public boudoir secrets never before visible, prove that the old taboos were crumbling.

JULES CHERET
A La Magicienne

1875; Chaix, Paris;
35 x 49 in / 88.9 x 122 cm

Although Chéret pioneered the concept of using skimpily-dressed sylphs as an advertising device, he could draw fully-clothed women equally well. Here, he promotes a store calling itself "At the Magician's"—undoubtedly for its ability to whip up enchanting custom-made women's dresses and suits.

❶❶❹

JULES CHERET
Aux Buttes Chaumont/Robes/ Manteaux/Modes

Ca. 1881; Chaix, Paris;
45 x 65 in / 114.4 x 165.2 cm

Maximizing a busy shopper's time, department stores like this one offered clothing for both women and children. You know you're in another century when a dress requiring yards and yards of material costs only 25 francs, and for less than four francs more you can outfit your child. Note the fashion dictates of the day: a waist cinched almost out of existence, high collar, and full-length skirt. That these encumbered women accomplished as much as they did is a tribute to their energy.

❶❶❸

RENE PEAN
A La Place Clichy/ Nouveautés de la Saison

1898; Chaix, Paris;
34 x 49¹/₂ in / 86.4 x 125.7 cm

The latest fashions of the 1898 Paris spring season are shown in this poster for a store which always engaged top artists to advertise its wares. Shoppers are also promised free bouquets of violets and mimosa from Nice.

❶❶❺

ANONYMOUS
Grand Bazar de L'Hotel-de-Ville

Ca. 1894; Emile Levy;
129¹/₂ x 39 in / 75 x 89 cm

An interesting view of the intermediate step between the open-air marketplace of yesteryear and today's shopping mall— a concentration of shops in an urban setting for the convenience of the shopping public. Merchandising was becoming highly sophisticated: Nearly all the world's major department stores, chain stores, and mail-order operations were founded in the last half of the 19th century, and huge bazaars like this one sprang up in every large town. They exposed shoppers—primarily women—to a variety of choices in a single area, encouraging impulse purchasers to spend more than if they had to travel distances from emporium to emporium.

❶❶❻

ANONYMOUS
Nouvelles Galeries

1908; Imp. Tourangelle, Tours;
43 x 59 in / 109.2 x 150.5 cm

To celebrate its anniversary, this Chartres department store is offering customers a free gift with every purchase priced higher than 15 francs. When a curious passerby stops a porter laden with the boxed gifts, the startled young man drops one, revealing its fragile contents. A charming illustration of early 20th-century retail marketing.

❶❶❼

JULES CHERET
Halle Aux Chapeaux/ Depuis 3F60

1892; Chaix, Paris;
32¹/₂ x 46¹/₂ in / 82.5 x 118 cm

The little girls and their mother trying on bonnets make a charming picture in one of Chéret's several designs for this hat store. Until the bicycle came along, shopping was one of the few activities allowed an unaccompanied woman outside the home.

❶❶❽

ANONYMOUS
Chaussures de Luxe P.D.C.

Ca. 1901; J. L. Goffart, Bruxelles;
12¹/₂ x 23¹/₄ in / 31.8 x 59 cm

Quick, fetch some shoes for the elegant customer! Even though her long skirt will hide all but the toes, she will appreciate their hand-sewn comfort and luxury.

❶❶❾

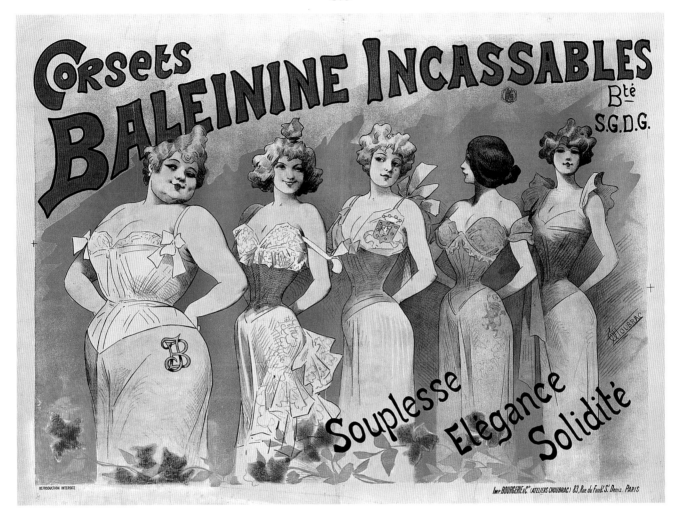

ALFRED CHOUBRAC
Corsets Baleinine Incassables

Ca. 1894; Bourgerie & Cie., Paris;
51 x 37 in / 129.5 x 94 cm

The bevy of models is meant to convince us that any woman—short, tall, thin, or plump—would benefit from wearing this brand of corset whose stays are made of unbreakable whalebone for "softness, elegance and long wear." No wonder the textile industry was humming: After the corset, it took a camisole, blouse, petticoats, and ankle-length dress before the wearer was ready to face the outside world.

❶❷⓿

GASTON NOURY
Les Corsets Le Furet

Ca. 1896; Affiche Atlas, France;
39 x 54 in / 99 x 137.1 cm

As integral to a Belle Epoque woman's toilette as her brush and comb was the corset that cinched her waist, smoothed her hips, and, depending on its cut, confined or enhanced her bosom. This brand, worn by a model in a classic cheesecake pose, boasts of being elegant, soft, and sanitary.

❶❷❷

ANONYMOUS
Corset du Médecin

Ca. 1895; Delaroche, Lyon;
23 x 30½ in / 58.4 x 77.5 cm

This "doctor's stretch corset" makes a welcome promise: a nicely rounded figure that doesn't compromise comfort. According to the explanation, the design features elastic inserts running down the sides which offer several advantages over traditional whalebone stays: They allow the wearer to fasten the corset herself and also provide a more natural, less exaggerated silhouette—all while aiding proper breathing and digestion! The doctor-inventor goes unidentified as does the graphic artist. But from the circular framing device and decorative pattern based on peacock feathers, it's clear that the artist was an admirer of Mucha and his Art-Nouveau style.

❶❷❶

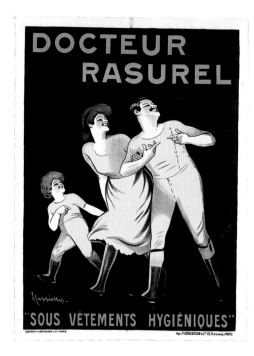

LEONETTO CAPPIELLO
Docteur Rasurel/ Sous Vêtements Hygiéniques

1906; Vercasson, Paris;
47½ x 63 in / 120 x 160 cm

Introduced in 1892, one-piece undergarments known as union suits gained wide popularity for a time. Here, they are advertised in an upbeat design of a happy family by Cappiello, who could always be counted on to put his subjects in motion and in a cheerful state of mind. Unsurprisingly, he was asked back to do a few more posters for the company.

❶❷❸

Sports & Recreation

Traditionally, women participated in sports only peripherally. In the first place, it was not considered ladylike to sweat. As a saying of the period held, "A woman never 'perspires', she 'glows.'" In the second place, athletics were considered risky—to the maiden's hymen and to the matron's child-bearing apparatus. Thus the reason for women's riding side-saddle. And you can imagine the hullaballoo the bicycle seat must have caused!

And when it came to professional contests, women were, at best, enthusiastic spectators. But this bastion, too, began to yield to feminine determination in the closing years of the 19th century. Tennis led the way in allowing women to participate; field hockey, basketball, and auto racing followed. In the first Olympics, held in 1896, no women were invited to participate; but in the second Games in 1900 this situation was corrected, and the first women's gold medals were earned in tennis and golf.

The freedom to participate in sports—in user-friendly clothing—and to attend sports events on an equal basis with men became another step along the way toward women's better futures.

PAL (JEAN DE PALEOLOGUE)
Patin-Bicyclette
Richard-Choubersky

Ca. 1898; Paul Dupont, Paris;
37 x 50 in / 94 x 125.5 cm

Somewhere between a roller skate and a scooter, this strange little contraption was obviously an invention being introduced to the public. No surprise that it never caught on, although skateboarding, a century later, might be considered a distant relative. The sight of the attractive and innovative "skater" on her miniature wheels is enough to bowl over a more conventionally bladed gentleman.

❶❷❹

ALBERT A. GUILLAUME
Palais de Glace

Ca. 1896; Charles Wall & Cie, Paris;
15³/₄ x 24 in / 40 x 61 cm

Customarily inclined to the simple linear approach and broad humor of a professional caricaturist, Guillaume takes an unusual departure to portray two skating women with tender flattery. As with dancing, it was common—and perfectly acceptable—for two women to skate together at the time.

❶❷❺

►

H. C. FORESTIER
A Game of Golf

Ca. 1898; Société Suisse d'Affiches Artistiques, Genève;
28¹/₂ x 37¹/₂ in / 72.4 x 95.2 cm

Women in Europe were pursuing golf as early as 1567 when Mary Queen of Scots was reproached for playing on the grounds of Seton House too soon after her husband's death. (American women were equally avid; the first U.S. Women's amateur tour took place in 1895, only a year after the USGA was founded.) This late 19th-century golfing scene, with its missing top panel of letters, was a poster in all likelihood for an elegant resort destination. As the rest of the mixed foursome waits for the player to complete her fairway shot, the caddy watches intently. Imagine what taking off that hat could do for her game!

❶❷❻

H.C. FORESTIER. DEL.

+C ForESTiER

SOCIÉTÉ SUISSE D'AFFICHES ARTISTIQUES (A. N) GENÈVE.

DANIEL DE LOSQUES (DAVID THOROUDE)
Marthe Régnier/Petite Peste

Ca. 1906: Imp. Ch. Wall, Paris;
15 x 22¹/₂ in /38.1 x 57.2 cm

At the beginning of the 20th century *le tennis* was so much *le thing* that it made its way off the lawn and onto the stage. Well into the 1920s, uninspired playwrights of country-house comedies could jumpstart the action with the line, "Tennis anyone?" In this small poster for the touring production of a Paris comedy smash, de Losques uses a caricaturistic style to announce that Marthe Régnier stars in the racquet-wielding title role of Petite Peste. Régnier was a reigning favorite of the Paris comic stage who delighted theatergoers with her vivacious, intelligent, tomboyish portrayals. So successful was she that in her 1911 divorce settlement from Abel Tarride, her actor-playwright husband of 14 years, she was ordered to pay him alimony—$80 a month for life. The judgment was unprecedented at the time, and it's still unusual today.

❶❷❼

GEORGES MEUNIER
Jardin de Paris/Montagnes Russes Nautiques

1895; Chaix, Paris;
33¹/₄ x 49 in / 84.1 x 123.8 cm

Wavering between calling this water slide a "nautical rollercoaster" with a Russian flavor and "the chutes of Niagara," the amusement park played it safe by giving the amusement both appellations. Three young girls, out on their own but not quite plucky enough to try it, wave a boatload of daredevil friends back to shore.

❶❷❽

►

CLEMENTINE-HELENE DUFAU
Pelote Basque

Ca. 1903; G. De Malherbe, Paris;
42 x 57¹/₂ in / 106 x 146 cm

The sport of jai-alai was formally introduced to Paris at the 1900 Olympics; this poster announces the opening of a court in the suburb of Neuilly. The artist was a painter and muralist who demonstrated a firm grip on composition and a feeling for color and mood in her rare forays into poster design. Here, she reassures women who might be timid about doing anything socially unacceptable that this newly introduced spectator sport is suitable for them to attend.

❶❷❾

1893; Chaix, Paris;
34½ x 48 in / 87.6 x 122 cm

❶❸⓿

JULES CHERET
Palais de Glace

Chéret executed several posters for this popular establishment, always with a delightful young woman in the spotlight, accompanied by the shadowy figure of a gentleman in the background. What we learn from all the designs is that women were able to enjoy indoor skating in full street clothes, including elaborate hats, coats, and capes.

▶

1900; Chaix, Paris;
34 x 48 in / 86.4 x 122 cm

❶❸❷

1896; Chaix, Paris;
33¼ x 48⅞ in / 84.5 x 124.2 cm

❶❸❶

ABEL FAIVRE
Chamonix

1905; J. Barreau, Paris;
29¹/₂ x 41¹/₂ in / 75 x 105.5 cm

The figure in this P.L.M. Railway promotion for winter sports in Chamonix takes absolutely no heed of the advice given French women by the vice-president of the Dauphin Ski Club in a publication of the period: "For skiing, hair should be very simply pulled back and tucked under a hat: no clever little curls, no complicated twists. In the wind how would they hold up? Skiing, in the mountains and valleys, with its intoxicating speed and freedom is a sport, a true sport, and something quite different from parlor games or passing flirtations." Faivre, however, is interested in appeal, not athletics, and it's difficult to resist his snow bunny.

❶❸❸

Travel

A great many travel posters were directed at women because, with their new economic clout, they were now often the ones to make the decisions about where to travel for recreational purposes. The advent of railroading in the 1830s had a profound effect on the French public's summer travel plans: Paris became almost deserted as everybody took a train to the coast, and seaside resorts became a big business. Women had a new reason to buy travel clothes and accessories and the opportunity to select a destination not only agreeable but fashionable in their social circle.

The stay-at-home image which many men harbored about their wives and daughters was rapidly fading away. Women were determined to see the world—and posterists did their best to make it appear agreeable, fun, and rewarding.

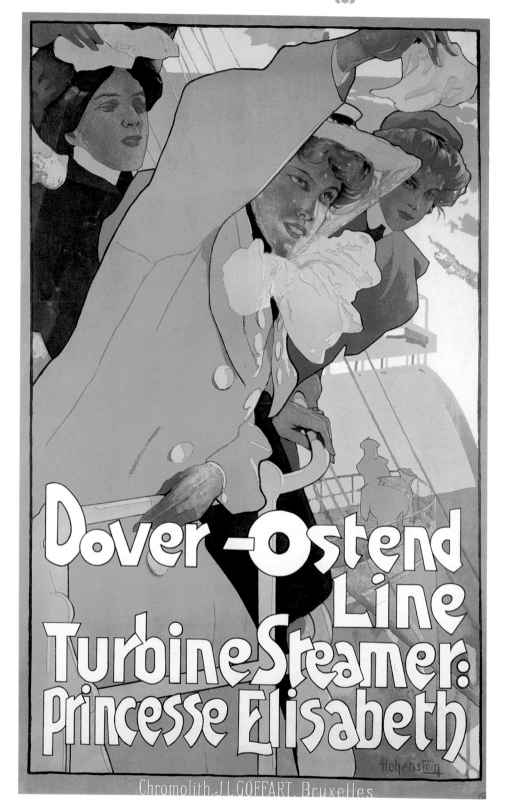

ADOLFO HOHENSTEIN
Dover-Ostend Line

Ca. 1900; G.L. Goffart, Bruxelles;
24¹/₂ x 38¹/₂ in / 62.2 x 97.8 cm

In this poster for a channel-crossing service between England and Belgium, Italian designer Hohenstein shows us the new woman, traveling unaccompanied by a man. She's not quite alone—that's her maid behind her, and the younger figure in red could be her daughter—but she will be responsible for handling the landing's logistics solo. The artist does a fine job creating a late-afternoon feeling: Golden tones, falling shadows, and the play of fading light on the central figure's face all combine to set the twilight mood.

❶❸❹

►

ADOLFO HOHENSTEIN
Monaco

1900; Ricordi, Milano;
31¹/₂ x 46¹/₂ in / 80 x 118.2 cm

To attract visitors for the 1900 season, the little Riviera municipality is staging a Spring motorboat show and racing meet. The invitation comes from a crisply-attired young woman at the helm of a handsome craft. Almost unthinkable!

❶❸❺

H. GRAY (HENRI BOULANGER)
Train-Scotte

Ca. 1900; Courmont Freres, Paris;
36 x 50 in / 91.5 x 127 cm

The advertised attraction, a bus with attached coaches to serve on short routes which have no rail connection, was in operation between Courbevoie-Neuilly and Colombes (Seine), and the manufacturer wanted to find more business with this poster. This curious means of transportation is safe and comfortable enough for women to enjoy, and Gray draws our attention to it through the backs of two fashionably dressed passengers about to board. They look—and we follow their gaze.
❶❸❻

JULES-ALEXANDRE GRÜN
Le Touquet/Paris-Plage

Ca. 1910; Imp. Cornille et Serre, Paris;
29 x 40 in / 73.8 x 108.8 cm

Advertising the northern line of the French national rail, Grün depicts the coastal resort of Le Touquet as an ideal family destination. By perching the mother and child on a hilly spot, he is able to include much of what a vacationing family might desire—beach, golf, wooded walks—in the view. It seems strange that the figures in a railway poster would be pointing to a passing airplane, but perhphaps they're waving at Papa out for a joyride. A fine, late poster from Grün, who is better known for his fun-loving images of Montmartre nightlife.
❶❸❼

►

GEORGES REDON
Boulogne S. Mer

1905; E. Marx & Cie, Paris;
29 x 42 in / 73 x 106 cm

The belle of the surf, 1905 style, invites you to a seaside resort. The poster lists the area's attractions at the bottom. This is an instructive glimpse of bathing attire acceptable to the period, exposing only the arms and the legs below the knees.
❶❸❽

LOUIS TAUZIN
Vichy

1911; F. Champenois, Paris;
30 x 42 in / 76.2 x 106.7 cm

An evocative view of this
famous spa at the height of the
season, with the fashionable
set promenading full force
outside a well-illuminated
casino. There are certainly men
here, but in the light of dusk
well-dressed women are seen
strolling alone or with their
young daughters and gathering
in groups of two or three.

140

GEORGES ANDRIQUE
Calais

Ca.1910; Lucien Serre & Cie, Paris;
24¹/₂ x 39¹/₂ in / 62.2 x 100.5 cm

This French railway poster for a
destination on the English
Channel coast highlights the
city's bustling port. A charmingly
sturdy young woman with
cheeks reddened by the brisk air
hauls her mast and sail home
after a satisfying morning's
catch. The whole image is just
the thing to make a land-locked
citizen yearn for salt air.

139

ANONYMOUS
Chemin de Fer du Nord/ Saison d'Eté

Ca. 1896; Courmont Frères, Paris;
37 x 54 in / 94 x 137.2 cm

Ladies in their best summer
finery enjoy the pleasure of the
season in Boulogne—one of
the many vacation spots
to which the Railway of the
North stands ready to
convey them.

141

Entertainment

Entertainment establishments traditionally catered to the family trade. Circuses, minstrel shows, vaudeville in the U.S., the British music hall, and the café-concert in France were geared to men and women equally, if not always to children. A Sunday afternoon ritual for the folk of Paris was to journey to the dance halls set up in former windmills atop the *butte* of Montmartre to dance and drink wine.

The Moulin Rouge opened in 1889. With Montmartre home to as many artists as cabarets and music halls, it's not surprising that the caliber of entertainment posters was so high. Grün lived in the bohemian quarter and depicted the stock characters of its silly revues without equal. Toulouse-Lautrec spent his most productive years at a studio on rue Caulaincourt, just a stroll away from the night spots he haunted.

The 1890s, however, brought both exploitation and emancipation. On one hand, new for-men-only places developed which appealed primarily to male prurience; on the other hand, it now became much more socially acceptable for women to attend cabarets and revues where they formerly would have felt conspicuous and out of place. In fact, some establishments used posters to indicate that a woman could enjoy an evening's entertainment out on her own without jeopardizing her reputation in any way.

GEORGES MEUNIER
Bullier

1895; Chaix, Paris;
34¹/₂ x 48 in / 87.6 x 122 cm

At first glance, the sheer elan of the design makes us assume it is one of Chéret's inspired revelries. Indeed, Meunier was an admirer and disciple of the master, and most of his poster work was done at the printing plant where Chéret reigned supreme. Perhaps a trifle less airy than some of Chéret's nymphs, and with her feet firmly on the ground, this cavorting joy-seeker takes second place to no one when it comes to having herself a ball.

❶❹❷

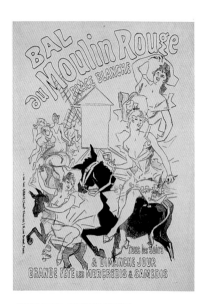

JULES CHERET
Bal du Moulin Rouge

1889; Chaix, Paris;
17¹/₄ x 25 in / 43.8 x 62.9 cm

This is Chéret's preliminary design for the poster announcing the opening of the Moulin Rouge, the cabaret which introduced that quintessential French innovation, the cancan. To attract customers, promoters Joseph Oller and Charles Zidler conceived of having some of the troupe parade in front of the place on donkeys before the show as Chéret depicts. Such stunts quickly became unnecessary: Reports of frilly feminine underthings revealed in the cancan's frenzy soon had all Paris flocking to the big red mill in droves.

❶❹❸

►

JULES CHERET
Tivoli/ Waux-Hall

1880; J. Chéret, Paris;
34 x 48 in / 86.4 x 122 cm

The Tivoli was located in a district with several trade schools and commercial establishments that supplied its predominantly young trade. Between 1872 and 1885 Chéret prepared several posters for the place. Here, a reveler in red and three other characters, all in costume for a masked ball, invite us to join the fun. Masked balls were the rage—nearly every cabaret, café-concert, and music-hall held them at least once a week.

❶❹❺

JULES CHERET
Elysée Montmartre/ Bal Masqué

1890; Chaix, Paris;
15¹/₂ x 22 in / 39.4 x 55.8 cm

One of the big Paris dance halls advertises by showing a couple enjoying themselves with abandon. One of Chéret's assets as a posterist was the way he gave his figures motion; there is a swing and a rhythm in his revelers that sweeps us right along with them.
It is hard to imagine one of Chéret's figures as a household drudge or seamstress; they seem to exist only for the moment, heedlessly bound for pleasure alone. The posters make you forget everything mundane—and therein lies the master posterist's greatest talent.

❶❹❹

PAL (JEAN DE PALEOLOGUE)
Folies-Bergère

Ca. 1896; Paul Dupont, Paris;
42 x 29¹/₂ in/ 106 x 74.9 cm

In the seven years Pal spent in Paris, the city's best known music-hall availed itself of his services at least a dozen times, recognizing his superior talent for showing women performers at their best. In this case, however, it's not the showgirls but the patrons who are being used to attract customers. Elegant and apparently out for the evening on their own, these two women assure prospective visitors of the showplace's high repute.

❶❹❼

◄

JULES CHERET
Olympia/
Montagnes Russes

1893; Chaix, Paris;
34¹/₄ x 48 in / 87 x 122 cm

As if her infectious exuberance wasn't enough, the scampering beauty clashes her cymbals to announce the opening of a new music-hall. The Olympia was built as an adjunct to an amusement ride calling itself "Russian Mountains"—a roller-coaster— which had been operating there for the past five years (see no. 128). It was made part of the Olympia, which also featured stage revues and musical plays. Chéret's hedonistic sprite sets the tone of the place eloquently.

❶❹❻

JULES-ALEXANDRE GRÜN
Réunis/ 58 rue Pigalle

1901; Chaix, Paris;
34 x 48 in / 86.4 x 122 cm

The carefree cocotte advertises a cabaret on Rue Pigalle, with two of Grün's previous posters for revues on the wall behind her. Grün lived in the bohemian quarter of Paris and frequented its many cafes and bars. Trained in decorative arts, he started to design their interiors and stage decors and soon was also producing posters. His revelers express the very mood of the Parisian tenderloin, light-headed and insouciant, with fun occupying every thought. The women especially exude an aura of charm with a hint of naughtiness that is Grün's own.

❶❹❽

Performing Arts

There was a time when the stage was so male-dominated that all roles were played by men. Major female stars were virtually unknown until Sarah Bernhardt became a dazzling international celebrity. Powerful enough to include classic male roles such as Hamlet in her repertory, she was also the first—in 1893—to own and operate her own theater, thus overcoming the stubbornly-held public opinion that consigned all actors to the lower class. With Bernhardt in the lead, other female stars emerged. Even motion pictures—the newest form of show business, which made its debut in Paris in December of 1895—had women in it from the very start.

The performing arts were perhaps the most natural place for women to show their talents to a wide public, and, ultimately, they would bring women a greater degree of popular fame than any other endeavor. The posters for productions and individual female performers—pioneering actresses, singers, dancers, and musicians—seem to anticipate this development with their enthusiastic depictions.

EUGENE GRASSET
L'Odeon

1890; G. de Malherbe & H. A. Cellot, Paris;
32 x 47¼ in / 81.3 x 120 cm

For the proper young woman of the Belle Epoque, theater-going—as well as virtually all other social and recreational activities—invariably involved a chaperone. In Grasset's design, this is expressed most eloquently: the young woman wistfully scanning the audience, the older one sternly watching. The image struck such a responsive chord that the printing firm used it later to advertise its lithographic skills, replacing the theater program with its own promotional copy.

149

MANUEL ORAZI
L'Hippodrome

1905; Société d'Impressions d'Art Industriel, Paris;
15½ x 23½ in / 39.3 x 59.7 cm

The Hippodrome was originally an open-air arena for equestrian sports and games; in 1905, it was covered with a roof so it could be used in any weather. The advertised event recreates a barbarian invasion featuring a flamboyantly bedecked horse ridden by a pagan princess. Orazi places her front and center in all her saber-rattling splendor.

150

►

HUGH PATON
Madame La Présidente

Ca. 1894; Louis Gallice, Paris;
24 x 35½ in / 61 x 90.2 cm

In the established system of monarchies, it was not unusual for a queen to take the reins of government—but would that be possible in a democracy? From the scenes depicted in this poster for a comic operetta by a designer who has a fine eye for expressions it seems that the question was answered in a humorous affirmative. Madame President appears to be taking her role seriously, but everyone else in the production is having a jolly good time.

151

ALPHONSE MUCHA
Gismonda

1894; Lemercier, Paris;
29 x 84 in / 73.7 x 213.4 cm

For Mucha, proponent of Art Nouveau, woman was a subject of reverence, even worship, and nowhere did he express it more eloquently than in his very first poster for the immortal actress Sarah Bernhardt. *Gismonda* was a biblical period piece whose Palm Sunday procession in the third act allowed Mucha to clothe the actress in a gown of Byzantine opulence and to give her a worshipful expression. At this time, when Paris billboards were dominated by Chéret's scampering sylphs and Toulouse-Lautrec's caricatures of the demi-monde, Mucha's meticulously drawn paean to women's spirituality struck a fresh note which launched a new chapter in poster art. With more than 100 posters to his credit, Mucha created only three or four that do not feature one of his idealized female subjects.

ABEL FAIVRE
Logiz de la Lune Rousse

Ca. 1895; Minot, Paris;
31 x 47 in / 78.7 x 119.4 cm

The completed poster with text advertises
the stage play *The Inn of the Russet Moon*,
a satire on the goings-on in a ramshackle
country place where the merry concierge
obviously doesn't hesitate to use binoculars
and a stool to spy on guests. Wonderfully
caricatured by Faivre, the figure is what the
French call *une jolie laide*—roughly translated
as "so ugly she's beautiful"—and the complete
opposite of the artist's charmer in no. 133.

①⑤③

GEORGES ROCHEGROSSE
Louise

1900; Ed. Delanchy, Paris;
25 x 33 in / 63.5 x 83.8 cm

A skilled illustrator, Rochegrosse honed his
technique on a number of books by literary
giants of his time: Theophile Gautier, Gustave
Flaubert, Victor Hugo, and others. He was
also house artist for the magazine *La Vie
Parisienne*. Here, he shows his mettle by
creating a tender, romantic lovers' tryst on a
height above a city, suffusing the whole scene
in a blue mist—a good way to promote a
sentimental musical by Gustave Charpentier.

①⑤④

EMILE BERTRAND
Cendrillon/J. Massenet

1899; Devambez, Paris;
23¹/₂ x 31¹/₄ in / 59.6 x 79.4 cm

For Massenet's musical version of Cinderella Bertrand evokes an eerily haunting twilight mood, animated by a fairy directing a flock of geese. Art-Nouveau ornamentation throughout the design brings the elements of this admirable composition together in a memorable image.

❶❺❺

MAURICE LELOIR
Cigale/J. Massenet

1904; Devambez, Paris;
21¹/₂ x 35 in / 55 x 89.9 cm

In this poster for a ballet based on La Fontaine's fable of the grasshopper and the ant, Leloir illustrates the frigid fate of the generous Cigale who has given away all of her worldly goods to a poor friend. Knocking at the door of the thrifty Mme. Fourmi to escape the cold, she is turned away and dies in the cold. So chilly is Leloir's color scheme and design that snow covers even the title letters. Jules Massenet was one of the most popular composers of his day, producing dozens of operas, operettas, ballets, chorales, and individual compositions. This full-length work, choreographed by Mariquita, had its premiere February 4, 1904 at the Opéra-Comique to benefit the company's orchestra, chorus, and stage crew.

❶❺❻

ALBERT G. MORROW
The New Woman

1894; David Allen & Sons, London;
20 x 28 in / 50.8 x 71.2 cm

This satire by English playwright Sydney Grundy concerns the attempts of three society women to explore the new trends in vogue at the end of the 19th century. The results are comic: Smoking only makes them sick; a light-hearted flirtation backfires by becoming deep love; and forays into uplifting intellectual pursuits turn hilarious. The work had a successful London run of 173 performances but closed in New York after less than two months. Whether or not Grundy himself regarded the feminist movement as a joke, he expressed society's opposition to it with eloquence and humor. For many women of the era, the way to emancipation entailed many a false and awkward step; the play and its poster serve as reminders.

157

◀

CHARLES LEANDRE
Le Mariage

1900; Chaix & G. Malherbe, Paris;
34 x 49 in / 86.4 x 124.5 cm

With text, this was a poster for a stage play about marriage; Leandre depicts the happy union in glowing terms, with the gentleman tenderly affectionate, the lady radiantly lovely and submissive, altogether a perfect ideal. This type of image was Leandre's specialty: Although he worked for several journals, did landscapes and occasional posters, his forte was flattering portraits. This endeared him to socialites who commissioned pictures of their families, particularly children, certain in the knowledge that they would be captured at their best, and the pursuit provided Leandre with his most reliable source of income.

158

A. TRINQUIER-TRIANON
Folies-Bergère/ Les Demoiselles du XXe Siècle

Ca. 1896; Charaire, Paris;
30 x 38 in / 76.2 x 96.5 cm

The Folies-Bergère prepares its customers for what they may expect from young women in the upcoming 20th century—not surprisingly, more of the same allure that its chorus girls had been offering for the past decade. When this most famous of Paris cabarets opened its doors in 1869, it presented variety programs including animal and circus acts, similar to American vaudeville. It was not until 1886 that its policy changed to concentrate on a line of show girls presenting various dances and specialty numbers in more or less revealing costumes. This proved to be a far bigger attraction, from which the management would never deviate.

159

JULES CHERET
Les Muscadins

1875; Chaix, Paris;
32½ x 46 in / 82.5 x 116.8 cm

The muscadine was a dance named for muscatel, a potent fortified wine; hence, the Muscadins are merrymakers addicted to wine, dance, and happy times. This is also apparent in Chéret's upbeat design for this revue, one of his earliest preserved color lithographs.

161

PAL (JEAN DE PALEOLOGUE)
Les Fêtards

1897; E. Delanchy, Paris;
23 x 31½ in / 58.4 x 89 cm

The Palais Royal was an early version of a shopping mall—an arcade with a number of stores, a bistro or two, and even a theater, which on this occasion was presenting a light musical revue. Pal comes through, as usual, with a delectable dancing damsel, obviously one of "the roisterers" of the title.

160

▶

PAL (JEAN DE PALEOLOGUE)
Olympia/Brighton

1893; Paul Dupont, Paris;
30½ x 48 in / 77.4 x 122 cm

The Olympia opened in Paris in April of 1893 as the first establishment to call itself a "music-hall"—a term borrowed from British vaudeville which soon made its way into French vocabulary. From the start, the Olympia exploited feminine allure for all it was worth; whatever its various revues were called, they always featured beautiful girls in revealing costumes. A full 15 years before Florenz Ziegfeld thought of glorifying the American girl, the display of sex appeal on stage was in full swing in Paris. Pal, freshly arrived from London, was a perfect choice to create one of the Olympia's first show posters. His well-proportioned, realistically drawn beauties projected a sensuality no other posterist could match.

162

MANUEL ORAZI
Olympia/
Rêve de Noël

1899; Lemercier, Paris;
43³/₄ x 58¹/₂ in / 109.8 x 148.6 cm

This revue at the Olympia featured Liane de Pougy, an entertainer who became notorious for sexual exploits among the cream of society, allegedly including a royal personage or two. The Olympia was quick to cash in on any performers with such reputations, knowing that notoriety added a measure of titillation to any talent.

❶❻❸

LEONETTO CAPPIELLO
Polaire/Le P'tit Jeune Homme

1903; Vercasson, Paris;
38¹/₂ x 53 in / 97.8 x 134.6 cm

Having demonstrated a talent for capturing, in a few bold strokes, outstanding characteristics of people in his home town of Livorno, Cappiello arrived in Paris in 1903 and turned to caricature to support himself. Published in popular magazines, his drawings of Parisian celebrities quickly led him to receive commissions from the theater. Here, he advertises a vehicle for a lively stage personality, Polaire. Originally from Algiers, she was born Emilie Marie Bouchaud and attracted attention as a cabaret singer at the age of 15; she made her way to the musical comedy field, where she proved to be an accomplished comedienne. The advertised piece, in which the bosomy performer was disguised as a young man, was produced at the Bouffes Parisiens theater in the 1903 season.

164

GEORGES DOLA (EDMOND VERNIER)
La Chauve-Souris

1904; Ch. Wall & Cie, Paris;
23¹/₂ x 31¹/₂ in / 59.6 x 80 cm

For this staging of the classic Johann Strauss operetta, Dola chose to depict Prince Orloffsky's ball from the second act. (Orloffsky is a "trouser role," traditionally played by a woman.) This was the first time Paris saw this internationally acclaimed work, which by rights should have been introduced there 30 years earlier, as it was based on a French piece in the first place. It seems that in 1872, Johann Strauss visited Paris and saw a stage play by Messrs Meilhac and Halevy titled *Le Reveillon*. He immediately approached the authors for the rights to put music to the piece, but they refused, hoping to sell the idea instead to their own favorite French composer, Jacques Offenbach. Strauss went home to Vienna and transformed the play into the operetta *Die Fledermaus*, which first saw light in 1874; because of the dispute with the authors, however, Strauss did not permit it to be performed in France. Thirty years of legal wrangling ensued until finally, in 1904, by which time both Strauss and Meilhac had died, Halevy consented to have the hallowed operetta presented in a French version.

165

JULES CHERET
Folies-Bergère/ Loïe Fuller

1897; Imp. Chaix, Paris;
33 x 47³/₄ in / 83.8 x 121.3 cm

In this poster advertising
Fuller's appearance at the
Folies-Bergère Chéret departs
from his usual red, yellow and
blue palette to capture the
dancer's presentation in all its
shifting colors and swirling
volumes. The pose is more
formal than the *Danse du Feu*
design, but the overall
treatment is perhaps
even more dazzling.

1 6 6

JULES CHERET
Folies-Bergère/ La Danse du Feu

1897; Chaix, Paris;
34 x 47¹/₂ in / 86.4 x 120.6 cm

Loie Fuller's meteoric rise to
fame is one of the oddest
success stories of the 1890s.
Coming from a small
Midwestern town in the States,
Fuller wanted a stage career;
accordingly, she studied singing,
dancing and acting, and started
getting some roles in the
theater. In one play, she noticed
how the spotlights, with
various color filters, created a
rainbow effect on the material
of her dress. Fascinated, she
experimented with the effect,
eventually working up a
specialty dance wearing
diaphanous materials on which
the colored lights played with
dazzling results. The act was
only moderately successful
when she tried it on the New
York stage in 1892, but she
booked an overseas tour, and
Paris loved the "fire dance"
beyond her wildest
expectations. Wisely, she made
the city her home from then
on, creating ever wilder light
shows that presaged
psychedelic laser shows by
three-quarters of a century. A
dozen or so of the best artists
of the day attempted to
capture her kaleidoscopic
gyrations with varying degrees
of success. Chéret, for whom
sprightly movement was
standard, came perhaps closer
than anyone to doing her
justice with this design.

1 6 8

JULES-ALEXANDRE GRÜN
Loïe Fuller

1901; Chaix, Paris;
42³/₄ x 62¹/₄ in / 108.5 x 158.1 cm

The dancer shows off her
costume—yards of dazzling
fabric which, in rapid motion
and with multi-colored lights
thrown at it, produced the
startling effects that captivated
Paris for years. It is interesting
to note that Grün, who was
quite adept at portraying brisk
movement, usually involving
frolicking merrymakers,
chose to show Fuller in a
stationary pose; possibly he
may have felt that so many
other artists had pictured her
as a swirl of color streaks that
he wanted to be different.

1 6 7

GEORGES DE FEURE (GEORGES VAN SLUITERS)
La Loïe Fuller/ Salome

1895; P. Leménil, Asnieres;
36¹/₂ x 50¹/₂ in / 92.7 x 128.3 cm

This poster shows Fuller taking on the ambitious project of combining her act with the story of one of the most notorious dancers of mythology. Where most artists attempted to capture the dancer's elusive magic by showing her as a blur amid a whirl of rainbow colors, de Feure uses a freeze-frame effect.

❶❻❾

►

LUCIEN METIVET
Eugénie Buffet/ Ambassadeurs

1893; Charles Verneau, Paris;
31¹/₂ x 47¹/₂ in / 80 x 120.7 cm

This is the earliest of three posters Metivet did for this chanteuse; in all cases, he puts her on ordinary Paris streets in the clothes of a Paris working girl, the persona she projected in her performances.

❶❼⓿

JULES CHERET
Lidia

1895; Imp. Chaix, Paris;
34 x 48¹/2 in / 86.4 x 123.2 cm

Using only her last name, Lily de Lidia graced some of the most popular music-hall stages of the day with her *gommeuse* (double-jointed) act. This poster, in a version that has letters at the top, announces Lidia's appearance at the outdoor Alcazar d'Eté. Chéret depicts the *artiste* almost life-size in a half-length view that's rare for him. Her expression is winsome, the creamy expanse of her decolletage appealing, and the overall design full of movement—from the sweeping ribbons of her hat to the swaying letters of her name.

❶❼❶

LUCIEN METIVET
Eugénie Buffet

1894; Charles Verneau, Paris;
20³/4 x 53 in / 52.8 x 134.6 cm

Other than the fact that the Buffet poster on the previous page (no. 170) depicts her facing right on a snowy day and this one has her facing left on a mild evening, the two images of the Parisian song stylist are much the same. She originally used this portrait as an announcement of her appearance at the Cigale. Then, as she went on to other engagements, she had it revised as a personal poster with her name large at the top and the subscript "dans son repertoire réaliste." Finally, as here, it became a decorative panel with no text at all. Buffet was quite popular in the intimate cabaret, preferring to forsake glamour and elaborate stage effects in favor of singing about common people and ordinary subjects in a down-to-earth "realistic" style.

❶❼❷

PAUL BERTHON
Sarah Bernhardt

1901; Bourgerie, Paris;
19¹/2 x 25¹/2 in / 49.5 x 64.8 cm

Berthon was a romanticist whose style was best suited to decorative panels. He produced about 60 of them, in fact, in contrast to his handful of posters for poetry books and art shows. This is his most famous lithograph, a portrait of Sarah Bernhardt in the title role of *La Princesse Lointaine* ("The Faraway Princess") which she first played in 1894. In this design Berthon transformed her costume tiara with its flowery jeweled garland into real irises framing her idealized face. As always with Berthon, the colors are the gentlest of pastels, and he has worked out the lacy pattern on her dress with great care.

❶❼❸

DANIEL DE LOSQUES (DAVID THOROUDE)
Marthe Régnier

Ca. 1909; Ch. Wall, Paris;
15³/4 / x 23¹/2 in / 40 x 59.6 cm

After studying law and taking a job as a legal clerk, de Losques became attracted to the theater as well as to art. During a ten-year period starting in 1904, he created a number of posters for plays and individual performers. When World War I broke out, he enlisted as a pilot and was killed in aerial combat in the second year of the war. In this poster, he has Régnier, a popular comic actress (see no. 127), assume a stage pose from an unidentified play.

174

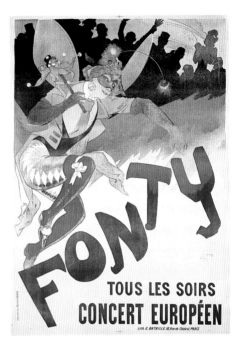

GEORGES DE FEURE (GEORGES VAN SLUITERS)
Fonty

Ca. 1894; G. Bataille, Paris;
36 x 50¹/2 in / 91.5 x 128.2 cm

Another of de Feure's enigmatic women, this masked performer wears an odd winged costume that makes it difficult to fathom what her act is really about. The Concert Européen was that Paris phenomenon, a *café-concert*: not just a restaurant, not just a theater, but an intimate bit of both. This one opened in 1872 and operated until 1948, so the formula must have been successful; many of the best performers in Paris got their breaks there, including Damia, Mayol, Max Dearly, and Yvette Guilbert.

176

EMILE LEVY
Nouma-Hawa

Ca. 1889; Imp. Emile Levy, Paris;
15³/4 x 23¹/4 in / 40 x 59 cm

In every traditionally male profession female pioneers sooner or later dared to break through. Even lion-taming. Quite a few circus patrons must have gone to see Nouma-Hawa for the sheer novelty of a woman among the big cats in the ring.

175

ALPHONSE MUCHA
Zdeňka Černý

1913; V. Neubert, Praha;
44 x 74½ in / 111.2 x 189.2 cm

During Mucha's sojourn in Chicago in 1906, he stayed with the family of compatriot Černý, a music teacher. There were three daughters, all trained by their father in music from infancy. Milada, the eldest, gave piano recitals at ten. Zdeňka, the next in line, became proficient enough on the cello to plan a European concert tour by age 14. And Marcela, the youngest, favored the viol. At the time Zdeňka was setting up her trip to Europe for the 1914-15 season, Mucha was long since gone from Chicago and living back in his home country; as a favor to his former hosts, however, he agreed to create a poster for the young virtuoso. As it turned out, the tour had to be canceled when war broke out in Europe during the summer of 1914.

❶❼❼

Events

Not surprisingly, posters announcing charity balls indicate that these events were eagerly awaited highlights of the Paris social season. But the number of posters for fairs, exhibitions, and celebrations featuring women is proof that at the end of the 19th century, Parisian women were avidly interested in cultural and intellectual activities as well.

The years between 1894 and 1899 saw the phenomenon of the Salon des Cent, highly anticipated showings of posters and prints. They took place at 31 rue Bonaparte in the exhibition hall of *La Plume* magazine, a publication devoted to graphic arts whose marketing arm issued special editions of these works. The posters announcing these shows often took women as their subject, and in posters for many art exhibitions women are depicted casting their critical eyes over the work on display. Obviously, their opinion was now given weight and respect. No longer willing to accept their fathers' and husbands' ideas about taste, women were developing their own and imposing their imprint on public events.

JULES CHERET
Blanc et Noir/
5e Expon.

1891; Chaix, Paris;
16 x 17¹/₂ in / 40.6 x 44.5 cm

Before motion pictures, there were
numerous attempts to provide
entertainment by means of
projection—from ordinary shadow
plays to elaborate presentations with
slides and "magic lanterns." This
poster advertises a program of
projected images, usually a series of
humorous drawings or photographs
which, when projected in sequence,
told a simple amusing story. One of
Chéret's high-spirited young women
does the inviting, and appropriately
for the photography of the period,
the design is in black and white.

❶❼❽

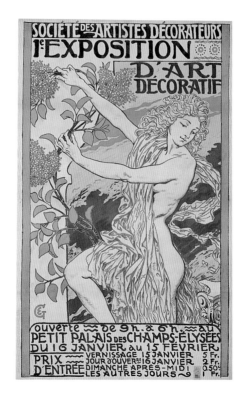

GASTON NOURY
Pour les Pauvres

1892; Herold & Cie, Paris;
39 x 54¹/₂ in / 99 x 138.4 cm

Two charming women enjoy a
ride at the Tuileries in the
name of charity. Each season
brought several events whose
proceeds went to various
charities in Paris; some of
them were regular, such as the
famous "Bal des petits lits
blancs" for a children's
hospital, others were arranged
for worthy causes as needed.
Often they turned out to be
glittering affairs with
prominent public figures in
attendance. This particular
event is a benefit for the poor
of France and Russia.

❶❼❾

EUGENE GRASSET
1e Exposition
d'Art Décoratif

1893; G. de Malherbe, Paris;
31 x 50¹/₂ in / 78.8 x 128.2 cm

This poster was for the first
annual show of decorative arts,
the beginning of a movement
which culminated in 1925 with
a widely acclaimed exhibition
that introduced Art Deco as a
major trend in a wide field of
applied arts. At this early stage,
veteran designer Grasset
represents Art Deco as a
lightly draped nude beauty
manipulating some flowering
branches, hinting at decorative
art's preoccupation with
themes from nature as
ornamental elements.

❶❽❶

ANONYMOUS
Première Exposition/ Photographie

Ca. 1895; Camis, Paris;
38 1/2 x 51 in / 97.8 x 129.5 cm

So many technological milestones had been achieved in the closing days of the 19th century that it's hard to remember that photography was already some six decades old in 1895: Daguerre had patented his "daguerrotype" in 1835, and the Lumière Brothers, already successful as manufacturers of photographic equipment, were about to take a giant step forward with motion pictures. In this poster, a young woman—perhaps an early photojournalist—has mounted a camera on her bicycle handlebars so she can snap away while riding.

❶❽❶

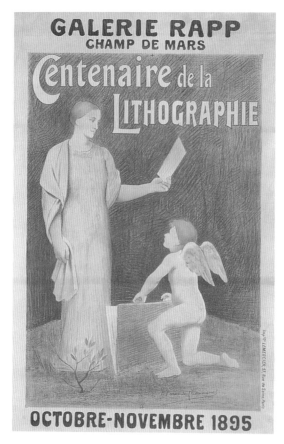

PIERRE PUVIS DE CHAVANNES
Centenaire de la Lithographie

1895; Lemercier, Paris;
37$^1/_2$ x 58 in / 95.2 x 147.4 cm

In the hands of this traditional painter, a design for a hundredth-anniversary exhibit of lithography becomes an allegorical scene in which the somewhat austere female figure represents the printing industry and the little cherub symbolizes the artists who labor in the lithography field. The use of mythical beings, predominantly female, was characteristic among the classically inclined designers.

❶❽❷

FERNAND GOTTLOB
2e Exposition des Peintres Lithographes

1898; Lemercier, Paris;
31 x 47 in / 78.7 x 119.2 cm

Gottlob's woman examining a display cradle of prints, though in shadows and seen from the back, creates a portrait in absorbed concentration. The occasion is an exhibition of lithographic artists at the Salle du Figaro; the letters have not yet been added in this proof.

❶❽❸

►

PIERRE BONNARD
Les Peintres Graveurs

1896; A. Clot, Paris;
18$^1/_2$ x 25 in / 46.9 x 61 cm

With this poster Bonnard announces an exhibition of 32 prints by members of the group of painters calling themselves the Nabis— including Vuillard, Vallotton, and Bonnard himself. The design looks over the shoulder of a woman who is critically examining a print. In his poetic way Bonnard leaves the non-essentials vague; what we see clearly is the picture being looked at—not surprising since the exhibition was staged to publicize the limited-edition portfolio of prints being published at the same time.

❶❽❹

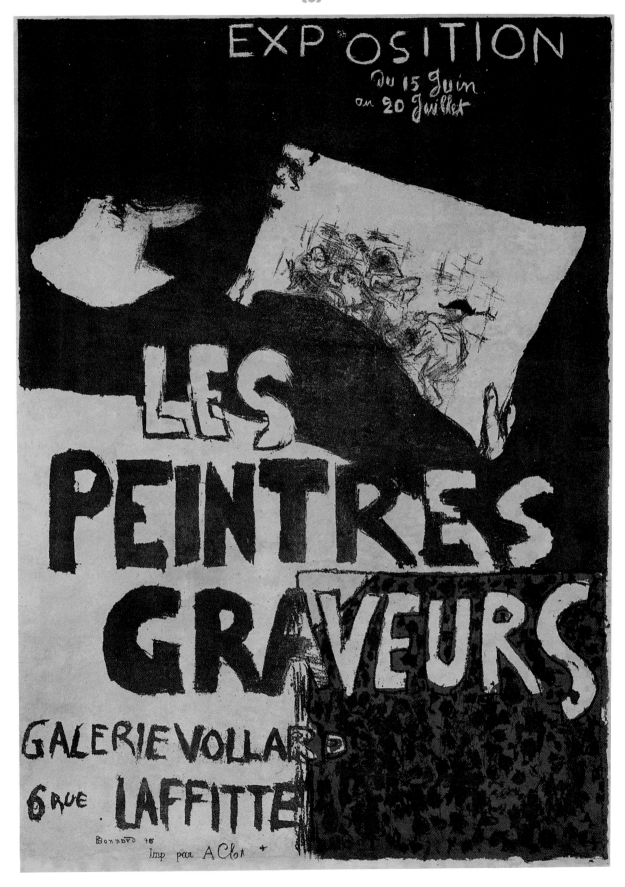

JULES CHERET
L'Andalousie au Temps des Maures

1900; Chaix, Paris;
34 x 49 in / 86.4 x 122 cm

The Spanish pavilion at the 1900 Paris World Fair featured an exhibition of Andalusian art from the time of the Moorish domination of the Iberian peninsula. The Moors were Islamic invaders from Africa who entered Spain around the year 700, remaining in power until they were decisively beaten at Granada in 1492. For his poster Chéret must have felt this winsome Spanish dancer would be more appealing than an illustrated history lesson.

❶❽❺

E. CHARLE LUCAS
L'Exposition du Théâtre et de la Musique

1896; Chaix, Paris;
13¼ x 32¼ in / 33.3 x 56.5 cm

To announce a four-month exhibition of theater and music at the Palace of Industry, a woman in simple draperies holds up the classical masks of comedy and tragedy. A laurel branch representing awards for performing artists completes the design.

❶❽❻

▶

GEORGES LEROUX
Exposition Universelle/ Palais de l'Optique

1899; Charle Verneau, Paris;
23½ x 31¾ in / 60 x 80.6 cm

By simply leaving the paper blank and highlighting the woman's face and arms, Leroux made the globe she holds seem luminous. The allegorical figure represents the spirit of progress, and the globe stands for the optical industry in this poster for the optics pavilion at the Paris World Fair of 1900. The building housing the exhibit was surmounted by a lighted dome, one of the fair's most spectacular sights.

❶❽❼

ANONYMOUS
Donaldson Fair

1913; Donaldson Litho, Newport, Kentucky;
20 x 30 in / 50.7 x 76.2 cm

A benevolent, nurturing allegorical woman—impeccably coiffed and dressed—invites the public to inspect the prize livestock, produce, and flowers at a county fair in Newport, Kentucky.

❶❾⓪

HENRI BELLERY-DESFONTAINES
Liège/Exposition Universelle

1905; Eugene Verneau, Paris;
34 x 46 in / 86.4 x 116.8 cm

As dignitaries prepare to open a world's fair in the Belgian city of Liège, an allegorical figure hovers behind them to give the event her blessing. The turn of the century was the era of grand expositions in major world cities. With scientific and technological developments coming in rapid succession, there always seemed to be a reason to celebrate progress in one field or another, and these fairs were the perfect vehicle to showcase technical innovations commercially.

❶❽❽

HENRI J. DETOUCHE
22e Exposition des Cent

1896; Chaix, Paris;
16¹/₂ x 25 in / 42 x 63.5 cm

In this odd and intriguing poster announcing the 22nd Salon des Cent, the woman is so fascinated by the wallpaper pattern of swans that she is caught in an unguarded moment trying to mimic them. Perhaps she wants to cast a shadow on the wall—a popular parlor pastime of the era.

❶❽❾

►

PAL (JEAN DE PALEOLOGUE)
Théâtre de l'Opéra/1er Bal Masqué

1899; R. Chardin, Paris;
44¹/₄ x 62¹/₄ in / 112.3 x 158.1 cm

The grand balls at the Opera were the highlights of the Paris winter season; anyone who aspired to be recognized as a member of high society simply had to be seen there. Traditionally, there were four such balls in the pre-Lenten weeks; this poster is for the first of the 1900 season. Pal, who did several of these designs, shows two fetching women in beautiful gowns. They have won the attention of a guest in Pierrot costume and doubtless many others.

❶❾❶

EUGENE GRASSET
Salon des Cent/ Exposition E. Grasset

1894; G. de Malherbe, Paris;
15¹/₂ x 23¹/₂ in / 39.4 x 59.6 cm

For his solo exhibition at the Salon des Cent, Grasset offers a capsule description of his work: His subject is usually a woman, seen as soulful, spiritual, sensitive and intense, and flowers are a recurring motif. A very insightful self-assessment.

❶❾❸

ALPHONSE MUCHA
Salon des Cent/ XXme Exposition

1896; F. Champenois, Paris;
17 x 25 in / 43.2 x 63.5 cm

"The Salon of the Hundred" was a small gallery on the premises of the magazine *La Plume* where promising designers displayed their work. The publication's marketing arm, Editions d'Art, also issued these posters and decorative panels in various editions, often on quality paper as art for the home. The bottom half of these posters—there were 43 in all—is normally filled with text. Legend has it that Mucha, who habitually filled every iota of space with decoration, was still working on this design when he was visited by *La Plume* editor-in-chief, Leon Deschamps, who insisted on taking the relatively unembellished artwork as is, declaring it to be a masterpiece. Indeed, Mucha's woman perfectly embodies an artist in a moment of inspirational rapture.

❶❾❷

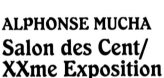

E. ROCHER
Salon des Cent

1895; Bourgerie & Cie., Paris;
17¹/₂ x 24 in / 44.5 x 61 cm

The woman is examining a print with intensely critical concentration—she might be an art student or even a painter herself. We don't know who the designer was, but at least he signed his (or her) name to this well-arranged composition in sepia tones.

❶❾❹

►

HENRI DE TOULOUSE-LAUTREC
Salon des Cent/ Exposition

1896; Bourgerie & Cie., Paris;
16¹/₄ x 24 in / 41.3 x 60.3 cm

According to poster lore, this elusive design for the 1896 Salon des Cent international group exhibition depicts a woman whom Toulouse-Lautrec glimpsed briefly while on board a ship sailing from Le Havre to Bordeaux; smitten, he pursued her all the way to Portugal without success. He did, however, manage to get a photograph of her, and on the basis of it, executed first a lithograph and then this poster. Like many Salon des Cent posters, it has nothing to do with the subject of posters per se, but it creates the kind of striking and memorable image that epitomizes the very best poster design.

❶❾❺

ANDREW K. WOMRATH
Salon des Cent/ XXVe Exposition

1897; printer not shown;
15 x 21¹/₂ in / 39.4 x 54.6 cm

Andrew Kay Womrath was an American artist who studied in New York, London, and Paris. This is his only known poster, showing a woman leafing through some prints while a man admires a vase. She is dressed conventionally enough, while the man, judging by his Van Dyke and floppy cravat, is either an artist or would-be bohemian.

❶❾❻

ADOLPHE L. WILLETTE
Salon des Cent/XXVIme Exposition d'Ensemble

1897; Chaix, Paris;
17¹/₂ x 22¹/₄ in / 44.4 x 56.5 cm

A pert temptress covers her bared breasts as the knife-wielding brute who has cut her bodice straps runs off. An offbeat, slightly naughty drawing by Willette, a preeminent political cartoonist and caricaturist who was a successful painter before he became interested in drawing and lithography at the age of 30.

❶❾❼

LOUIS RHEAD
Salon des Cent/ Exposition Louis Rhead

1897; Chaix, Paris;
14¹/₄ x 33 in / 36.8 x 83.8 cm

For his own exhibition in Paris, Rhead shows an artist in a fascinating dress and cape of his own design. She wears a triumphant wreath of laurel, and the daubs on her palette carry out Rhead's three-color scheme. The thin white outline around the figure gives her an aura suggesting that she is not meant to be a real woman but rather an idealized representation of artistry.

❶❾❽

Decorative Art

Decorative panels were sold for home use by enterprising print dealers who either used the image part of a poster without its text or had the artist produce a special design just for the purpose; then they printed the design in multiple copies, just like a poster, and sold it for a few francs. Sometimes it worked the other way around: Clients might take a design sold as a decorative panel and turn it into a poster by adding advertising text.

The Parisian printer F. Champenois added mightily to his coffers by marketing works of his star producer Alphonse Mucha this way. But while Mucha's designs usually led off the illustrated Champenois catalogues, many lesser names also contributed images. Artists such as Paul Berthon were known to print their own decorative panels. Series that personified various seasons, flowers, gemstones or moods as women allowed the designers to give especially free rein to their imaginations.

PRIVAT LIVEMONT
La Vague

1897; Van Leer & Cie, Amsterdam;
27¹/₂ x 20¹/₂ in / 69.8 x 52 cm

One of the acknowledged masters of Art Nouveau, this Belgian lithographer and graphic designer made women virtually his sole subject, treating them with a tender delicacy. One of the feminine characteristics he habitually emphasized was long, flowing tresses, and here he carries his worship to a virtual apotheosis, seeing an ocean wave as a manifestation of woman's mystique—deep and restless, yet eternally soothing.

❶⑨⑨

PAUL BERTHON
Les Eglantines

1900; Chaix, Paris;
25¹/₂ x 19¹/₂ in / 64.8 x 49.5 cm

The subject is the wild rose, but it hardly matters, as it is the flower gatherer who engages our attention; we derive our enjoyment from the way she enjoys the beauty and fragrance around her. Berthon always interprets women with an exquisite finesse—in terms of their spirituality rather than their physical substance.

❷⓿⓿

PAUL BERTHON
Les Boules de Neige

1900; Chaix, Paris;
25¹/₂ x 19¹/₂ in / 64.8 x 49.5 cm

Of all the posterists who also designed decorative panels, Berthon was perhaps the best qualified to do a series on flowers personified as women since his women are so flower-like—delicate creatures, so light as to be nearly ethereal, seen in the softest of focus and tinged with the gentlest of pastel hues. The flower here is a variety of white rose; the woman a shy, soulful spirit passing by in our dreams.

②①❶

PAVL BERTHON

ABEL TRUCHET
Le Quadrille

1900; Eugène Verneau, Paris;
33 x 25½ in / 83.8 x 64.8 cm

This is a decorative panel—
mass-produced art for the home—with
an interesting view of the cancan from
the rear. From this vantage all we get is a
hint of the swirl of white petticoats, yet it
is enough to communicate the zest and
energy of this French specialty. The title
given to the artwork goes back to the
name of the original dance for four
couples from which the cancan evolved.

❷⓿❸

ABEL TRUCHET
Les Danseuses

1900; Eugène Verneau, Paris;
33 x 25½ in / 83.8 x 64.8 cm

This nicely conceived scene in a well-
patronized cafe shows women dancing
together, a normal practice at the time.
Truchet was primarily a painter, but he
also mastered the techniques of
illustration, etching, and lithography and
produced a few posters of undoubted
merit. He found his inspiration among the
habitues of Montmartre, and this is a fine
example of the results.

❷⓿❹

◀

PAUL BERTHON
Lace

Ca. 1900; printer not shown;
14½ x 18½ in / 36.8 x 47 cm

This portrait of a young woman wearing
an intricate lace collar is one of Berthon's
most elusive designs. Holding a branch of
lunaria (whose ovals are echoed in the lace
pattern), she is pensive and profound,
gazing at us without a trace of coquetry,
yet creating an ineluctable feminine charm
with her innocent sincerity.

❷⓿❷

EUGENE GRASSET
L'Eventail

1900; Chaix, Paris;
33¹/₂ x 51¹/₂ in / 85.1 x 130.8 cm

Wielding an unusually
large fan, the young
woman is either cooling
herself on a summer's
day or flirting—or both.
In any case, her gaze
is intriguing.

EUGENE GRASSET
Le Parasol

1900; Chaix, Paris;
37 x 50 in / 85.1 x 130.8 cm

Protected against the elements, the young woman peeks out from under her protective canopy in a most charming manner.

❷⓪❻

Artists' Biographies

GEORGES ANDRIQUE

A native of Calais, Andrique studied with several notable painters and became a specialist in landscapes and marine scenes. He was a member of the Société des Artistes Français and exhibited at its prestigious Salon several times from 1927 on, winning an honorable mention in 1929.

MARCELLIN AUZOLLE (1862-1942)

Something of a mystery, Auzolle left a legacy of about two dozen posters which show him to be a skilled craftsman who carefully composed his designs for good effect. Of his own life, however, there is nary a trace. Yet he became a part of poster history unwittingly, as he happened to be the one asked to produce a poster advertising the Lumière Brothers' original 1895 public show of their *cinématographe*—a milestone recognized as the true start of motion pictures as a medium of mass entertainment. In that memorable poster he captured the astonished reaction of several patrons— the first moviegoers in history—to the images on the screen in front of them. Indeed, expressions of people vividly portrayed at special moments seem to be Auzolle's specialty.

PAUL BALLURIAU (1860-1917)

Balluriau entered the field of graphic arts as a prolific illustrator for various magazines; one of them, *Gil Blas Illustré*, offered him the post of art director in 1897. His posters are comparatively rare, always carefully conceived and executed, designed to tell a story in visual terms.

ADRIEN BARRERE (1877-1931)

Barrère studied law and medicine but found his true calling when he turned to caricature at the age of 25; he had an uncanny common touch which made his images instantly recognizable and hugely appealing. He did dozens of posters, mainly for stage and film comedians, and worked often for the Grand Guignol Theater and early Pathé Company films.

HENRI BELLERY-DESFONTAINES (1867-1909)

Almost nothing is known about Bellery-Desfontaines personally but his brief life seems to have been extraordinarily busy. Along with a handful of posters, he left behind evidence of a successful career as a painter as well as a designer of sets, furniture, books, and typography. Both the 1897 and 1898 editions of the prestigious *L'Estampe moderne* carried an example of his color lithographs.

EMILE BERCHMANS (1867-1947)

Berchmans was a Belgian artist from Liège who had already attained some measure of success with his paintings before he turned to posters. He was a co-founder of the *Caprice Revue*, a periodical devoted to art and literature, and a member of La Libre Esthetique, an artists' society. His poster designs exude an aura of casual spontaneity that was achieved as a deliberate effort by a highly skilled hand.

G. BERNI

Only two posters of his have been found in the archives of the Bibliothèque National in Paris, and two or three others have turned up in hands of collectors, but no information about the artist has trickled down to posterity. In one or two of the known works, he approaches Pal in carefully drawn semi-nude female figures: the others are functional, workmanlike designs for commercial clients.

PAUL BERTHON (1872-1909)

Greatly influenced by Grasset, Berthon pursued a wide range of activities: book binding, ceramics, and illustration; in the end, he became attracted to posters and decorative panels. His posters are relatively rare: He created only a handful of them, mostly on subjects like books of poetry and art shows. It was in decorative panels where he excelled, producing more than 60 in a relatively short life span (he died at 37). They usually took a theme from nature—flowers, birds, landscapes—expressed by a woman. The symbolic females were always presented with great sensitivity, in soft shades of the gentlest pastels, soulful and somehow profoundly moving—a mannered, formal approach modified by tender compassion, exalting the spiritual aspect of female nature.

EMILE P. BERTAND

A painter and engraver active at the end of the 19th and beginning of the 20th century, Bertrand belonged to the Société des Artistes Français and showed his works at its Salons.

V. BOCCHINO

No information found.

PIERRE BONNARD (1867-1947)

With his subtle, introspective style, Bonnard seemed ill-suited to the needs of posters; indeed, his posters are few and rare. There is an aura of mystery in them—more is obscured than revealed, and a dark mood usually prevails. Yet even though he ventured into lithography rarely, preferring paintings, drawings and prints, Bonnard exercised considerable influence; it has long been held that it was he who induced his good friend Toulouse-Lautrec to try poster art, with spectacular results.

FIRMIN BOUISSET (1859-1825)

After studies at the Ecole des Beaux-Arts in Paris, Bouisset set out to become a portraitist; he specialized in children, even doing some murals for children's rooms for wealthy families. It was only natural that, when asked to design a poster for a major chocolate manufacturer, he thought of a little girl as a subject, coming up with a memorable, instantly recognizable trademark figure. Bouisset branched out into book illustration, calendar design, and other lithographic works, but nothing ever earned him such fame as his demonstration of the powerful commercial appeal of an adorable little child.

WILL H. BRADLEY (1868-1962)

The foremost exponent of Art Nouveau in America, Bradley was well-versed in all aspects of graphic arts: illustration, lithography, printing, and poster design. After working for journals including *The Inland Printer, St. Nicholas, The Chap Book,* and *The Century,* he started his own publishing venture, The Wayside Press, where he launched his own magazine, *Bradley—His Book.* In later years he became art director for *The Century, Collier's,* and *Good Housekeeping.* His work is characterized by decorative borders executed with minute care and precision, usually based on natural patterns like leaves or flowers.

GUSTAVE BRISSARD

Very little is known about this artist beyond the fact that he apparently hailed from the small provincial town of Bonny-sur-Loire and that he specialized in painting scenic views of the Seine and the environs of Paris. These were received well by the public and exhibited annually between 1877 and 1892 in the prestigious Salons of the Société des Artistes Français.

BRUN, CHARLES (1825-1908)

No information found.

LEONETTO CAPPIELLO (1875-1942)

A native of Livorno, Italy, this fine caricaturist came to Paris as a young man and liked the artistic atmosphere enough to settle there. He created something of a revolution with his simple linear approach and flat colors, ending the era of Art Nouveau's painstaking attention to detail and elaborate ornamentation. What his posters lacked in depth they more than made up for in showiness: exaggerations that rivet the eye to an absurd or incongruous feature which then leads to the advertising message. Most posters of the 1890s work leisurely; Cappiello intuitively recognized that with so many images competing for attention, the future in advertising would belong to whoever could deliver a quick punch and outshout the others. The new century's marketing strategies were to develop a whole new dynamism—and Cappiello started it all with a bang.

WILL CARQUEVILLE (1871-1946)

Carqueville studied art in Paris before returning home to Chicago to open a studio. From early on, he became involved with *Lippincott's,* a Philadelphia-based magazine of general-interest features and articles for family reading, and remained its house artist for most of his career. He patterned his designs to a great extent on Penfield, a fellow American posterist whose work he greatly admired: simple but eloquent linear drawings in flat colors, depicting scenes with an anecdotal flavor.

JULES CHERET (1863-1932)

Born in Paris, Chéret was sent to work as a printer's apprentice at age 13. Mastering the skills of lithography, still a crude and expensive printing technique, he refined and simplified the process until it finally became an economically feasible way of producing posters in color. After honing his talent in London, where lithography was at a more advanced stage, he returned to Paris and started creating posters, mainly for the stage, full of sprightly, lightly-dressed damsels—entirely at odds with the stodgy, static poster designs prevailing at the time. He created a virtual marketing revolution: On formerly gray Paris streets posters now dazzled passers-by with a profusion of dynamic images and bright colors. Chéret may not have been the first to discover that the image of a pretty girl will sell anything, but he certainly practiced the art assiduously, confirming its truth to all who followed. Prolific as well as successful, he prepared some 1,000 posters between 1858 and the first decade of the 20th century.

ALFRED CHOUBRAC (1853-1902)

Choubrac was one of the very few posterists who practiced their trade successfully before the golden Nineties. Educated in Paris, he started as a painter of military scenes in collaboration with his brother Leon, then branched out into caricature and illustrations for popular magazines before switching to scene design for theaters. It was only in the early 1880s that he finally joined the small but growing cadre of poster artists. In the first poster exhibition, held in 1884, the work of only three French designers was deemed worthy of inclusion: Chéret and the two Choubrac brothers. Alfred's debt to Chéret is apparent in his designs, but his approach is generally more illustrative and restrained.

HENRI J. DETOUCHE (1854-1913)

A native of Paris, Detouche started out in decorative crafts, designing furnishings and ornamental objects. He proceeded to paint in watercolors and pastels, exhibiting most of his work at the Salon des Humoristes. Still later, he went on to dry-point etchings and lithographs and even wrote three books. His forays into posters are quite rare.

GEORGES DOLA (EDMOND VERNIER — 1872-1950)

Vernier took his pseudonym from the town of Dole in eastern France where he was born. He left little biographical data behind, but it is known that he had his own studio in Paris where he produced a great number of posters, mostly for theatrical productions; later, he became one of the first to specialize in the fledgling field of motion-picture posters. He also executed a few paintings and collages. In his posters his approach is strictly illustrative, capturing vivid scenes from the advertised plays and movies.

CLEMENTINE-HELENE DUFAU (1869-1937)

Dufau studied at the Academie Julian where she sided at first with the naturalists, then turned to decorative styles and symbolism; painting remained her primary interest for the rest of her life. Her posters are quite rare and were mostly motivated by her desire to serve the cause of feminism. She was one of the followers of suffragette Marguerite Durand, and it was for her magazine, *La Fronde,* that she produced her most famous work, eloquently expressing women's desire to be led out of their inferior status to a brighter future.

ABEL FAIVRE (1867-?)

Coming from his native Lyon to study fine arts in Paris, Faivre started to get his paintings—mostly figure studies and portraits in oils—shown at major Salons in 1892. He was a good draftsman and sold a number of illustrations and cartoons to *Le Rire, Figaro,* and similar magazines.

L. LUCIEN FAURE (1892-?)

Other than Faure's output of a dozen or so posters, little is known about him.

GEORGES FAY (?-1916)

Almost nothing is known of this artist who was killed at the Front during World War I.

GEORGES DE FEURE (GEORGES VAN SLUITER — 1868-1943)

Van Sluiter was the son of a Dutch architect living in Paris. As a youth, he joined the ranks of symbolist painters, and his first watercolors were accepted in one of their exhibitions. He then branched out into designing tapestry, furniture, and stage decor; among his works was the interior of the famous Chat Noir cabaret. In the 1890s he came to posters, evolving a highly unusual style from elements of Art Nouveau, Oriental prints, and symbolism. His attitude to women was especially interesting: He portrayed them as enigmatic, with an inscrutable allure that borders on mystique; they are generally elegant but unapproachable, sometimes with a sly little smile that hints they are harboring secrets that they will not share with us. After 1902, despite the success of his posters, de Feure inexplicably went back to theatrical design. He remained at it for the rest of his life, including a 15-year sojourn in London.

HENRI C. FORESTIER (1875-?)

Forestier was born in Geneva, but came to Paris in his youth to serve as an apprentice to a woodcut artist. He learned the trade and in 1896 returned to Switzerland, where he began producing various graphic designs in several media, all with a decorative, personal character that gained him wide popular acceptance—especially his panels for the home. He also did theater decor and contributed drawings to magazines including *Le Sapajou, Le Passepartout,* and *Album Genèvois.* In 1903 the print dealer Sagot published a portfolio of his titled *Sujets de Chasse.* Four years later he turned primarily to serious painting.

P. GAUTIER

No information found.

EMILE G. GIRAN (1870-1902)

Born in Montpélier, Giran was educated in Paris; at age 20, he had already had a still life accepted in a major Salon, and from 1894 on he painted mostly boudoir scenes and interiors of cafes and similar establishments. He also created several successful posters, of which the one for the Folies-Bergère Bar became quite popular. There are not many of his works to be found because he regrettably died at the young age of 32.

FERNAND L. GOTTLOB (1873-1935)

With an innate talent for drawing, Gottlob sold his first lithographs while still in his teens and became a frequent contributor of illustrations, mainly caricatures, to several Paris journals. He also designed postcards and illustrated books for a living. His posters are rare and always interesting.

EUGENE GRASSET (1845-1917)

After studying architecture in his native Switzerland and even working for an architectural firm, Grasset decided at age 26 to move to Paris and devote himself to art. He tried ceramics, designed furniture, tapestry and jewelry, and worked in metals. In 1877 he turned to graphic arts and again covered the whole field, producing everything from book and magazine covers, postcards and illustrations, to postage stamps. Finally he started doing the decorative panels and posters which became his mainstay. His style was steeped in classical concepts, formal and almost austere at times, yet flexible enough to embrace contemporary trends.

HENRI GRAY (HENRI BOULANGER — 1858-1924)

Boulanger started out contributing illustrations and caricatures to magazines. In 1882 he joined the staff of *Paris s'Amuse*, then moved to the *Chronique Parisienne* for which he designed many covers. In 1888 he started working for *Paris-Noel*, designing costumes for leading cabarets as a sideline. For a time during the height of poster popularity, he dabbled in the field, using the pseudonym "Gray." His designs have a flair often approaching flamboyance, and he sometimes exploits feminine pulchritude to exalt a product or event.

JULES-ALEXANDRE GRÜN (1868-1934)

Like many posterists, Grün started painting as a hobby—mostly still lifes and portraits—but soon went on to selling illustrations to magazines to earn a living. Dwelling as he did in the bohemian quarter of Paris, he frequented local cafes and cabarets, and that led to his offering them his services for interior decor and stage sets. Happy with the results, the establishments began to commission him to produce posters for the shows they were staging. This is where his natural talent asserted itself. He had an uncanny ability to catch the carefree spirit of Paris nightlife: the flirtatious coquettes out for some fun, concupiscent gentlemen in ardent pursuit of them, comical gendarmes, and assorted street characters in quest of pleasure. Nearly all the women he showed in his posters are young, pretty, and out on the town, well aware of their attractiveness and determined to enjoy it to the fullest.

ALBERT A. GUILLAUME (1873-1942)

Showing a natural talent for caricature, Guillaume gravitated toward creating cartoons for humor magazines such as *Gil Blas Illustré, Le Gaulois, Le Rire,* and *Figaro Illustré*. A collection of his theatrical sketches was published when he was only 17. When asked to do posters, he at first emulated Chéret's style but gradually added elements of caricature until he found his own niche.

PAUL C. HELLEU (1859-?)

An exceptionally gifted student, Helleu came from his native Vannes to Paris to enter the Academy at age 15. He was at first attracted to ceramics, then went into portraits which earned him much admiration from other artists as well as the general public. He also ventured into graphic arts—etchings and lithography—with similar success. Becoming a renowned and fashionable society portraitist, he was invited outside France to work in Germany, England, and the U.S. His style was sometimes compared with that of the American artist Whistler.

RAOUL-EDWARD HEM

No dates are known for Hem, but he was born in the Paris suburb of Neuilly-sur-Seine and studied in the city itself with many fine artists including Flameng. During the first decade of the 20th century, he exhibited several series of lithographs at the Salon des Artistes Français.

ADOLFO HOHENSTEIN (1854-1928)

Hohenstein was a native of Germany but in 1889 he came to Milan, attracted by the chance to work for Ricordi, one of the best-known printing firms in Europe. Soon he was designing posters for a great variety of subjects. His approach, clearly influenced by the flowering of Italian art, was somewhat monumental, often with classic references or symbols; his specialty was a precise rendering of the play between light and shadow on faces or various surfaces.

CHARLES LEANDRE (1862-1930)

Leandre made a comfortable living as a portrait painter, proving especially adept at handling children; he also executed some landscapes. In graphic arts, he contributed illustrations to various magazines. His interest in posters was only marginal, but evidently he acquitted himself quite honorably when the occasion arose.

LUCIEN LEFEVRE

One of the best pupils of Chéret, Lefèvre was a prolific posterist who left behind a number of good works but scarcely anything about his life. He also produced a few portraits, some of which found their way into the Paris Salons of 1872 and 1873.

MAURICE LELOIR (1853-?)

This Paris-born painter and illustrator remains largely obscure despite his undoubted talents. His specialty seems to have been the creation of effective scenes with particular moods; this made him particularly adept at illustrating books. It was he who illustrated the original edition of *The Three Musketeers,* as well as a great many other well-known novels.

GEORGES P. LEROUX (1877-?)

Leroux painted figures and landscapes of great merit and was a member of the Société des Artistes Français; in 1930, he became a member of the Academy. In 1906, his paintings received the Grand Prix in an exhibition at Rome, and he earned much other recognition throughout his career. His posters are infrequent and rare.

EMILE LEVY (1826-1890)

Not well known for his posters, Lévy did, however, reach a fair measure of fame with his paintings. One of them was hung in the Luxembourg, others regularly earned major prizes in exhibitions (Grand Prix in Rome, 1854), and he was elevated to Knight of the Legion of Honor in 1867 for his contribution to art. He was especially good at portraits.

PRIVAT LIVEMONT (1861-1936)

Signing his name with a hyphen (although Privat was simply his first name), this Belgian artist was one of the pioneers of the decorous and richly ornamental Art-Nouveau style which became fashionable in the early 1890s. A fine painter, he became attracted to posters accidentally, having submitted a design for an art exhibit poster which won a prize; he then trained himself in lithography and created a number of attractive posters. Regardless of the poster's purpose he virtually always chose a woman with a classically beautiful face as his subject and portrayed her richly dressed and bejeweled or adorned with flowers. A special feature of his designs is a thin white outline around the women's figures, which tends to underline their purity and radiance, somewhat like a halo. This reverence for women and their exaltation in posters invites a comparison with Mucha and the notion that one may have been a follower of the other. In reality, however, the two artists developed independently of each other, on parallel tracks but in different countries, with Livemont having a slight edge chronologically but Mucha eventually surpassing him in universal appeal.

DANIEL DE LOSQUES (DAVID THOROUDE — 1889-1915)

Like many posterists of the era, de Losques was originally a magazine illustrator, but from 1904 to 1914 he was active in theatrical circles, producing many posters and other designs. He enlisted as a pilot in World War I and was killed in aerial combat. His chief influence appears to have been Cappiello, who also traveled the same path from caricature to the theater. Most of his designs take a light-hearted approach, portraying performers with a mild but always flattering amusement.

E. CHARLE LUCAS

Born Charles-Louis Lucas, the artist signed all his posters, including several for the Paris daily *Le Journal,* as E. Charle Lucas. Little else in known of him.

LUCIEN METIVET (1863-1932)

By trade an illustrator of magazines and books, Métivet once even won a world-wide contest announced by an American magazine, *The Century,* for an illustration announcing a serialization of a novel about Napoleon. His posters are few and have the general appearance of fine illustrations, executed objectively but with keen insight.

LEOPOLD METLICOVITZ (1868-1944)

Born in Trieste, the old city-state on the Adriatic, Metlicovitz was of Serbian ancestry but chose to live and work in Italy—mainly at Ricordi's renowned printing firm in Milan. Ambitious and a quick study, he mastered the art of lithography so well that he became the firm's technical director within a year of arriving there as a trainee in 1891. Thereafter, he produced a number of posters at a fast clip, evolving his own style, often quite grandiose in conception, but with a great sensitivity to the interplay between light and shadow which distinguishes all his work. His technique, which came to be known as "bourgeois realism," soon characterized much of Ricordi's poster output. It was especially useful in posters for stores selling stylish clothes at reasonable prices—elegance to which an average homemaker could aspire without having to bankrupt herself.

GEORGES MEUNIER (1869-1942)

Educated in both classical art and modern decorative trends, Meunier started in his native Paris as a painter, good enough to have his work exhibited in prestigious Salons. At 25, influenced by Chéret, he turned to posters. His designs are lively, often with a humoristic touch, but he stayed with them for only a short time; by 1898, he embarked on a new career as a book illustrator, which became his permanent livelihood.

MISTI (FERDINAND MIFLIEZ — 1865-1923)

A native of Paris, this painter and lithographer had already achieved a measure of Salon success with his paintings when he embarked on a poster career which kept him busy from 1894 until World War I. The bulk of his graphic work was done for the Pygmalion department store and for Dubonnet, in a style that owed much to Chéret but showed enough independent spirit to be artistically interesting.

C. MORIGET

No information found.

ALBERT G. MORROW (1863-1927)

An illustrator and painter of genre scenes and landscapes, the Irish-born Morrow studied at the Royal College of Art and exhibited at the Royal Academy from 1890. Joining the staff of the *English Illustrated Magazine* in 1884, he provided illustrations for numerous books and periodicals. He lived for some years in Sussex.

ALPHONSE MUCHA (1860-1939)

Born in a small town in Moravia which, at the time, was part of the Austro-Hungarian Empire and later became part of independent Czechoslovakia, Mucha grew up in an environment where the only available artwork could be seen in churches. But when he accepted a job in Vienna to paint scenery for a theater, he came into contact with fine-art circles and determined to join them. After studies in Munich and Paris, financed by a rich patron, he settled down in the French capital to produce a prodigious number of graphic works, mainly posters. He took the principles of Art Nouveau to greater heights than anyone before or after him, becoming virtually synonymous with the movement. His fame was greatly abetted by ardent supporters: publisher Leon Deschamps whose magazine *La Plume* tirelessly publicized his work; printer F. Champenois who reaped profits by marketing his work both to commercial clients and individual buyers; and Sarah Bernhardt who championed him in high society. More than 90 percent of Mucha's designs feature women, usually idealized and portrayed wearing exquisite gowns and jewelry, often against an ornamental background that functions as a halo. After visiting the U.S. for a time, Mucha returned permanently to his home country in 1910 and devoted himself to painting on nationalistic themes.

GASTON NOURY (1856-?)

No personal data seem to be available about this artist other than that he was born in Elbeuf and worked for many years as a book and magazine illustrator, draftsman and poster designer.

VACLAV OLIVA

No information found.

MANUEL ORAZI (1860-1934)

A native of Rome, Orazi spent most of his productive years in Paris as a graphic designer and decorator. He earned a living supplying illustrations to journals such as *Paris-Noel, Le Figaro,* and *L'Assiette au Beurre* and eventually secured a position as jewelry designer for the prestigious Paris store La Maison Moderne. In both paintings and posters, he favored somewhat exotic themes with Art-Nouveau overtones.

PAL (JEAN DE PALEOLOGUE — 1860-1942)

A genuine aristocrat, Pal came from a long line of Rumanian rulers whose ancestors helped to create the Byzantine Empire. But he had no ambitions to lead a nobleman's life, opting instead for commercial art. He worked for a time in London, mostly as a magazine illustrator. Then in 1893 he moved to Paris where he astounded the poster world with his realistic nudes and near-nudes selling everything from bicycles to kerosene lamps. He executed every curve of the female figure and every nuance of skin tone with meticulous attention, creating some of the most provocative temptresses that ever appeared on billboards. After seven years in Paris, however, he abruptly left for the United States where he found work mostly in the film and animation industries, creating only a few posters from time to time. He died in Miami.

HUGH PATON (1853-1927)

Paton was a Scot from Glasgow who spent most of his career as a painter and engraver in Manchester. He also visited the Continent on occasion and created some posters in Paris.

RENE PEAN (1875-?)

One of Chéret's most brilliant followers, who worked at the same printer as the master, Péan specialized in theater and cabaret posters from around 1890 to 1905. After being among the first to produce posters for the fledgling new movie industry, he faded into obscurity.

EDWARD PENFIELD (1866-1925)

Throughout the 1890s Penfield was closely associated with *Harper's* magazine, acting as art director and designing store placards to advertise the publication's monthly issues. His drawings are straightforward, executed with an economy of line and color; yet their seeming simplicity masks insinuating designs with a pervasive message: The magazine is read by the young, elegant set that is worth emulating. After leaving *Harper's,* Penfield created product posters using the same technique.

PIERRE PUVIS DE CHAVANNES (1824-1898)

Puvis de Chavannes was on his way to becoming an engineer when an illness sidetracked him to Italy where he became enchanted with classic arts and turned to painting. Mostly self-taught, he attained a great deal of fame and popularity. At the height of his powers he was asked to create murals for the Paris Pantheon, a project which consumed five years (1874-78). His posters are very few and very rare.

ETHEL REED (1876-?)

Best known as a book illustrator, Reed did most of her work for the Boston publisher Lamson Wolffe. When she ventured into posters—actually counter or window placards to advertise new books in bookstores—she proved to be a capable designer. Her clever, genteel images prompted several critics to term her the foremost woman poster designer in the U.S. Her productive years were confined to the last five years of the 19th century; she then married and left to live in England, apparently abandoning her career.

LOUIS J. RHEAD (1858-1926)

Born in England, illustrator and decorator Rhead created a name for himself as a top posterist only after settling in the United States at the age of 25. The decorator's taste is evident in most of his poster work, which often features fancy borders and ornamental elements. He had connections in England and France who commissioned posters from him from time to time, and all of these works became prized collector's items. He was the only posterist to have exhibits of his work in New York, Paris, and London during his lifetime.

GEORGES REDON (1869-1943)

Painting flowers was Redon's hobby, but like many young artists, he couldn't make a living at it and turned to illustrations and caricatures for various publications. He also became involved with posters, creating a number of designs for a short-lived experimental Montmartre theater named La Boite à Musique. Whatever the client, he could always be counted on to come up with an effective, eye-catching concept.

MANUEL ROBBE (1872-1936)

Robbe was known mainly for producing a great number of decorative prints in a bold, robust style that made them quite popular. His posters are rare and show a flair for composition in lively primary colors.

GEORGES ROCHEGROSSE (1859-1938)

Rochegrosse endeared himself to fine-art connoisseurs with meticulously realistic depictions of great moments in French history; for that, he earned a Legion of Honor medal and other prizes which enabled him to do illustrations for books of the finest contemporary authors. His poster designs have the aura of illustrations—well-planned scenes expressing specific moods and attitudes, executed with a fine sense of drama.

EDMOND A. ROCHER (1873-?)

A versatile artist from Issy-sur-Seine, Rocher was equally adept at illustration, lithography, poster design, and etching; he even published three collections of poems which he illustrated himself. But other than the evidence of his work, there is little information available about him.

AUGUSTE ROUBILLE (1872-1955)

Like many of his contemporaries, Roubille had ambitions to become a painter but drifted of necessity to drawing cartoons and caricatures for magazines such as *Le Rire, Le Sourire, Cocorico,* and even the German humor periodical, *Lustige Blätter.* He used his caricature style in his posters whenever possible, especially in a number of designs for small satirical and musical revues.

THEOPHILE-ALEXANDRE STEINLEN (1859-1923)

Born in Lausanne, Switzerland, Steinlen moved to Paris at age 22 to pursue a career in art. There, he met another Swiss expatriate, Rodolphe Salis, who published Steinlen's drawings in his magazine *Le Chat Noir* and let him do posters for his cabaret of the same name. With his warm, humanistic touch, Steinlen earned popular acceptance and contributed literally thousands of illustrations, cartoons and drawings to dozens of publications. In his poster work he often used his wife, daughter, and the family cats as models and showed a sensitivity to social issues of his day. In Steinlen's hands, women are seen mostly as ordinary working girls or homemakers, and his sympathy shines brightly in every one of his posters.

FRANCISCO TAMAGNO (1851-?)

Born in Portugal, Tamagno started his artistic career as a portrait painter. Around 1880 he came to Paris where he learned lithography, eventually working his way up to chief designer at the printing firm Camis. Creating theatrical playbills at first, he then graduated to posters for the firm's many clients, including railroads, bicycle manufacturers and distillers, before going independent. As a skilled portraitist, he recognized the value of famous faces and was one of the first to put the likeness of celebrities in his poster designs. His carefully-drawn images have a light touch and often abound in good humor.

LOUIS TAUZIN (1845-1914)

For 48 consecutive years (1867-1914), Tauzin's works—mostly landscapes and architectural paintings—were exhibited annually in Salons of the Société des Artistes Français. His forays into posters were infrequent, and it's hardly surprising that they conveyed the feeling of fine paintings. Because of his special talents, he was most often asked to produce posters for resorts, fine restaurants, and similar clients.

E. THELEM (ERNEST BARTHELEMY LEM — 1869-1930)

For some unknown reason, the artist used a shortened version of his middle name as his surname. He should not be confused with the caricaturist Jacques Lemaire (b. 1925) who signed his works "Lem."

HENRI THIRIET

Thiriet would have doubtlessly been considered one of the most celebrated exponents of Art Nouveau, with its stylized conventions and ornamental patterns, if only there had been enough posters of his to look at. He could rise to delightful impertinence when the occasion warranted it, but in general he produced pleasing posters for bicycles and other products. After a few years, he faded from the art scene without supplying any biographical data about himself.

HENRI DE TOULOUSE-LAUTREC (1864-1901)

An aristocrat by birth, Toulouse-Lautrec already showed a talent for drawing as a boy and later came to Paris to study art formally. He settled permanently in Montmartre, fascinated by its nightlife from which he drew most of his inspiration. He had an uncanny eye for facial expressions, gestures, and body language, which he caught with deadly accuracy and wit in drawings, sketches, and paintings. Already assured of widespread fame, Toulouse-Lautrec at 27 discovered lithography. It became his favorite means of expression, and over the ensuing ten years he produced some 400 lithographic masterpieces, of which 31 were posters. Most of his poster work depicts Paris nightclubs, cabarets, brothels, and bars, making wry comments about the habits, follies, and foibles of their colorful denizens. Yet with all his sharpness and keen perception, Toulouse-Lautrec never made caricatures to insult or demean but rather to awaken our own sensibilities and powers of observation.

A. TRINQUIER-TRIANON

No information found.

ABEL TRUCHET (1857-1918)

Truchet painted and created prints and etchings in the tenderloin district of Paris where he lived and found his inspiration; the bars, cabarets, and cafes of Montmartre were his home, and their habitués his subjects. His poster designs often showed women—from high-class ladies slumming to blatant streetwalkers plying their trade in the streets. He also liked to portray performers, dancers, singers, and chorus girls, always with a measure of tender compassion.

EUGENE VAVASSEUR (1863-?)

Vavasseur was a prolific contributor of humorous cartoons and drawings to half a dozen periodicals, using either his real name or the pseudonym "Ripp." Not surprisingly, his posters are conceived as scenes which could work well with a humorous caption underneath, drawn with a sure-fire eye for the comical.

ADOLPHE L. WILLETTE (1857-1926)

Already a successful painter, Willette at age 30 decided to pursue a new career in graphic design, mainly so he could publish political cartoons in satirical revues such as *Le Rire* and *Chat Noir.* He began publishing three journals of his own—*Le Pied de Nez, Le Pierrot,* and *La Vache Enragée*—and was one of the organizers of the Salon des Humoristes. His drawings abound in subtle humorous touches, revealing an artist with a keen eye and a sure grasp of design. Restrained by subject matter, the few posters he produced unfortunately do not let us fully appreciate his abundant talents.

MOSNAR YENDIS (SIDNEY RANSOM)

Giving a humorous twist to his signature as well as to his work, this caricaturist habitually signed his name backwards or used the initials M.Y.

Index

(Numbers refer to poster numbers)

A La Magicienne, 114
A La Place Clichy/Exposition de Blanc, 23
A La Place Clichy/Jouets Etrennes, 31
A La Place Clichy/Nouveautés de la Saison, 115
Absinthe Robette, 43
Affiches et Estampes Pierrefort, 35
Ah! Quand Supprimera-t-on L'Alcool?, 50
Aluminite, 11
Andalousie au Temps des Maures, L', 185
Andrique, Georges, 139
Anonymous, 5, 6, 12, 13, 16, 25, 40, 41, 91, 95, 107, 111, 116, 117, 119, 121, 141, 181, 190
Appareils & Accessoires Pour La Photographie, 27
Assommoir, L', 86
Auto Barre, 76
Automobile Club de France, 77
Aux Buttes Chaumont/Jouets!, 30
Aux Buttes Chaumont/Robes/Manteaux/Modes, 113
Aux Fabriques de Genève/E. Billard, 29
Auzolle, Marcellin, 76

Bains Douche Lyonnais, 40
Bal du Moulin Rouge, 143
Balluriau, Paul, 93
Barmaid of the 20th Century, 41
Barrère, Adrien, 65
Bazar de l'Hotel de Ville, 37
Bellery-Desfontaines, Henri, 188
Benzo Moteur, 22
Berchmans, Emile, 19
Berni, G., 37
Berthon, Paul, 173, 200, 201, 202
Bertrand, Emile, 155
Biscuits Lefèvre-Utile (also see Lefèvre-Utile Biscuits and Flirt), 59
Biscuits Pernot/Genève, 64
Blanc et Noir/5e Expon., 178
Bocchino, V., 58
Bonnard, Pierre, 89, 184
Bouisset, Firmin, 60
Boules de Neige, Les, 201
Boulogne S. Mer, 138
Bradley/His Book/June (1896), 106
Bradley, Will H., 82, 105, 106
Brissard, G., 71
Brun, Charles, 73
Bullier, 142
Byrrh, 44

Cacao A. Driessen, 53
Cacao Van Houten, 54
Café Malt, 57
Calais, 139
Cappiello, Leonetto, 14, 45, 49, 61, 96, 123, 164
Carqueville, Will, 103
Cendrillon/J. Massenet, 155
Centenaire de la Lithographie, 182
Chamonix, 133
Chap-Book, The/Being a Miscellany, 105
Chaussures de Luxe P.D.C., 119
Chauve-Souris, La, 165
Chavannaz, 50
Chemin de Fer du Nord/Saison d'Eté, 141
Chéret, Jules, 8, 22, 26, 28, 30, 32, 33, 42, 46, 81, 113, 114, 118, 130, 131, 132, 143, 144, 145, 146, 161, 166, 168, 171, 178, 185
Chocolat Klaus, 61
Chocolat Menier, 60
Choubrac, Alfred, 120
Cigale/J. Massenet, 156
Claudine, 83
Clinique Chéron, 39
Compagnie Française des Chocolats et des Thés, 55
Compagnie Singer Nähmaschinen, 16
Corset du Médecin, 121
Corsets Baleinine Incassables, 120
Corsets Le Furet, Les, 122
Crème Eclair, 52
Cycles & Accessoires Griffiths, 67
Cycles Automoto, 72
Cycles Buffalo, 73
Cycles Mentor, 71
Cycles Peugeot, 75
Cycles Sirius, 69

Danceuses, Les, 204
Delineator, The, 95
Demandez un Marra, 48
Detouche, Henri J., 189
Docteur Rasurel/Sous Vêtements Hygiéniques, 123
Documents Décoratifs, 87
Dola, Georges (Edmond Vernier), 165
Donaldson Fair, 190
Dover-Ostend Line, 134
Dufau, Clémentine-Hélène, 98, 129

Eclair, L', 93
Eau des Sirènes, L', 8

Ed. Sagot, 34
Eglantines, Les, 200
Elles, 85
Elysée Montmartre/Bal Masque, 144
Encre L. Marquet, 3
Estampe et L'Affiche, L', 89
Estampe Moderne, L', 88
Eugénie Buffet/Ambassadeurs (1893), 170
Eugénie Buffet (1894), 172
Eventail, L', 205
Eyquem, 17
Excellent, L', 51
Exposition de Blanc/à la Place Clichy, 24
Exposition du Théâtre et de la Musique, L', 186
Exposition Universelle/Palais d'Optique, 187
1e Exposition d'Art Décoratif, 180
2e Exposition des Peintres Lithographes, 183
22e Exposition des Cent, 189

F. Champenois/Imprimerie-Editeur, 36
Faivre, Abel, 133, 153
Faure, Lucien, 83
Fernand Clément & Cie, 68
Fêtards, Les, 160
de Feure, Georges (Georges van Sluiters), 35, 79, 169, 176
Fleur du Bouquet de Noce, 5
Fleurs de Mousse, 7
Flirt, 63
Folies-Bergère, 147
Folies-Bergère/La Danse du Feu, 168
Folies-Bergère/Les Demoiselles du XXe Siècle, 159
Folies-Bergère/Löie Fuller, 166
Fonty, 176
Forestier, H.C., 126
Formodol, 6
Fringilla, 82
Fronde, La, 98

Game of Golf, A, 126
Gautier, R., 10
Giran, Emile G., 62
Gismonda, 152
Gottlob, Fernand, 183
Grand Bazar de L'Hotel-de-Ville, 116
Grande Patisserie Lisboa, 62
Grasset, Eugène, 3, 78, 84, 149, 180, 193, 205, 206
Gray, H. (Henri Boulanger), 9, 69, 73, 136
Grün, Jules Alexandre, 1, 44, 137, 148, 167
Guillaume, Albert A., 64, 125

Halle Aux Chapeaux/Depuis 3F60, 118
Hammond, 18
Harper's/June/Thackeray (1911), 107
Harper's/May (1896), 101
Harper's/September (1896), 102
Helleu, Paul C., 34
Hem, R., 29
Hérold & Cie, 1
Hippodrome, L', 150
Hohenstein, Adolfo, 134, 135
Hysope des Alpines, 47

Inceste, L', 91

Jardin de Paris/Montagnes Russes Nautiques,
    128
Job, 2
Journal, Le, 96
Journal, Le/La Traite des Blanches, 90

Lace, 202
Lait Pur Stérilisé, 56
Lampe Belge, La, 19
Laveine/Enlève Encre, 4
Leandre, Charles, 158
Lefèvre, Lucien, 4, 57
Lefèvre-Utile Biscuits, 58
Leloir, Maurice, 156
Leroux, Georges, 187
Lévy, Emile, 175
Librairie Romantique, 84
Lidia, 171
Liège/Exposition Universelle, 188
Lippincott's/April (1895), 103
Livemont, Privat, 38, 43, 53, 54, 77, 199
Logiz de la Lune Rousse, 153
Löie Fuller, 167
Löie Fuller, La/Salome, 169
de Losques, Daniel (David Thoroude), 127,
    174
Louise, 154
Lucas, E. Charle, 186

Machines à Coudre Peugeot, 15
Madame La Présidente, 151
Marque Georges Richard, 78
Mariage, Le, 158
Marthe Régnier, 174
Marthe Régnier/Petite Peste, 127
Métivet, Lucien, 170, 172
Metlicovitz, Leopold, 7
Meunier, Georges, 51, 52, 128, 142
Michiels Frères, 38
Miss Träumerei, , 80
Misti (Fernand Mifliez), 31
Monaco, 135
Moriget, C., 27
Morrow, Albert G., 157
Motricine, 25

Mucha, Alphonse, 2, 36, 59, 63, 74, 87, 88,
    97, 152, 177, 192
Muscadins, Les, 161

New Home, La, 13
New Woman, The, 157
Nouma-Hawa, 175
Noury, Gaston, 122, 179
Nouvelles Galeries, 117
Nuyens's Menthe, 45

Odeon, L', 149
Olympia/Brighton, 162
Olympia/Montagnes Russes, 146
Olympia/Rêve de Noël, 163
Oliva, Václav, 109
Orazi, Manuel, 150, 163
Ovale, L', 9

Pal (Jean de Paléologue), 17, 21, 23, 66, 68,
    108, 110, 124, 147, 160, 162, 191
Palais de Glace (1893), 130
Palais de Glace (1896), 131
Palais de Glace (Ca. 1896), 125
Palais de Glace (1900), 132
Parasol, Le, 206
Paris-Almanach, 79
Pastilles Geraudel, 32
Pastilles Poncelet, 33
Patin-Bicyclette Richard-Choubersky, 124
Paton, Hugh, 151
Péan, René, 115
Pêcheurs Réunis, 65
Peintres Graveurs, Les, 184
Pelote Basque, 129
Penfield, Edward, 100, 101, 102
Petit Parisien, Le, 111
Petit Sou, Le, 99
Physique & Chimie Populaires, 81
Pianos Ortiz & Cusso, 14
Plaque Electra, La, 10
Plasson Cycles, 70
Polaire/Le P'tit Jeune Homme, 164
Poster, The, 112
Poster Calendar 1897, 100
Pour les Pauvres, 179
Première Exposition/Photographie, 181
Puvis de Chavannes, Pierre, 182

Quadrille, Le, 203
Quinquina Dubonnet, 46

Rayon D'Or, 21
Redon, Georges, 138
Reed, Ethel, 80
Repassage Au Gaz, Le, 12
Réunis/58 rue Pigalle, 148
Reverie (see F. Champenois/Imprimeur-
    Editeur)

Revue Blanche, La, 92
Rhead, Louis, 94, 104, 198
Robbe, Manuel, 70
Rochegrosse, Georges, 154
Rocher, E., 194
Roubille, Auguste, 20

Salon des Cent (1895), 194
Salon des Cent/Exposition (1896), 195
Salon des Cent/Exposition E. Grasset, 193
Salon des Cent/Exposition Louis Rhead, 198
Salon des Cent/XXme Exposition, 192
Salon des Cent/XXVe Exposition, 196
Salon des Cent/XXVIme Exposition
    d'Ensemble, 197
Sarah Bernhardt, 173
Saxoléine (1896), 26
Saxoléine (1900), 28
Scribner's/for Xmas (1895), 104
Société la Française, 66
Spratt's Patent Ltd., 20
Steinlen, Théophile-Alexandre, 39, 55, 56,
    86, 90, 99
Suc du Velay, 49

Tamagno, Francisco, 11, 47, 48, 72
Tauzin, Louis, 140
Théâtre de l'Opéra/1er Bal Masque, 191
Thelem, E. (E. Barthélemy Lem), 75
Thiriet, Henri, 15, 24, 67
Tivoli/Waux-Hall, 145
de Toulouse-Lautrec, Henri, 85, 92, 195
Touquet, Le/Paris-Plage, 137
Train-Scotte, 136
Truchet, Abel, 203, 204
Truth for April (1901), 108
Truth for July (1901), 110
Trinquier-Trianon, A., 159

Vague, La, 199
Vavasseur, Eugène, 18
Vichy, 140
Vin Mariani, 42

Waverly Cycles, 74
Willette, Adolphe L., 197
Winter Tales for Winter Nights/Sunday
    Press, 94
Womrath, Andrew K., 196

Yendis, Mosnar (Sidney Ransom), 112

Zdeňka Cerný, 177
Zlatà Praha, 109
Zodiac/La Plume, 97